CW01663044

En

Stitches

The MADEIRA Book of Embroidery Stitches

Jenny Bullen

First paperback edition
published 1990 by
Madeira Threads (UK) Ltd
ISBN 0-9516348-0-1

First published in hardback in 1990 by
A & C Black (Publishers) Limited
35 Bedford Row, London WC1R 4JH
ISBN 0-7136-3294-1

A CIP catalogue record for this book is available from the British Library

Line drawings by Peter Haillay
Photography by Peter Kinnear and Alphabet & Image

Typeset by Susan Higginson
Printed in Great Britain by BPCC Paulton Books Limited

Title page picture: Summer Garden – Marigolds, worked by Margaret Rivers. Calico has been used for the background, lightly washed with fabric paints. The embroidery is a combination of hand and machine stitching, the hand stitches including buttonhole and satin stitches to represent the flowers. Embroidered area: 7 x 4 inches (17.5 x 10 cm).

Contents

Introduction

Most of the stitches in this book are surface embroidery stitches: that is, they are all worked into the surface of the fabric. I have included two or three which could be called counted thread stitches, such as darning and Holbein stitch, because of their usefulness, and because I feel that they have their place among the rest of the stitches described. I have also included the basic machine embroidery stitches as they are so important in contemporary embroidery – even if one is not a machine embroiderer it is important to know as much about each part of the embroidery world as possible.

The first chapter includes a section on materials and equipment, how to begin and how to finish, which I hope will be helpful to those who are just beginning. The stitches themselves are illustrated with coloured photographs which help to show how the stitch should be worked, and under each stitch I have included, as well as basic instructions, suggestions on how to experiment by using different threads, altering the direction of the stitch, and working the stitch in varying sizes. It is not necessary to know how to work all the stitches in the book. It is more important to know a few stitches well and to know how to make them work. However, as well as some of the better known stitches, it is a good idea to try some of those that are less well known. Thorn stitch, for example, is a simple stitch and very versatile; some of the background filling stitches are quite beautiful, such as tete-de-boeuf, brick and cross, and exciting pieces of work can be made up solely using some of the large filling stitches, such as couched filling. There are, of course, other surface stitches not included in this book, which does not aim to be comprehensive. I have chosen those that I feel will be particularly useful to the embroiderer, whether a beginner or more advanced, wishing to extend his or her knowledge.

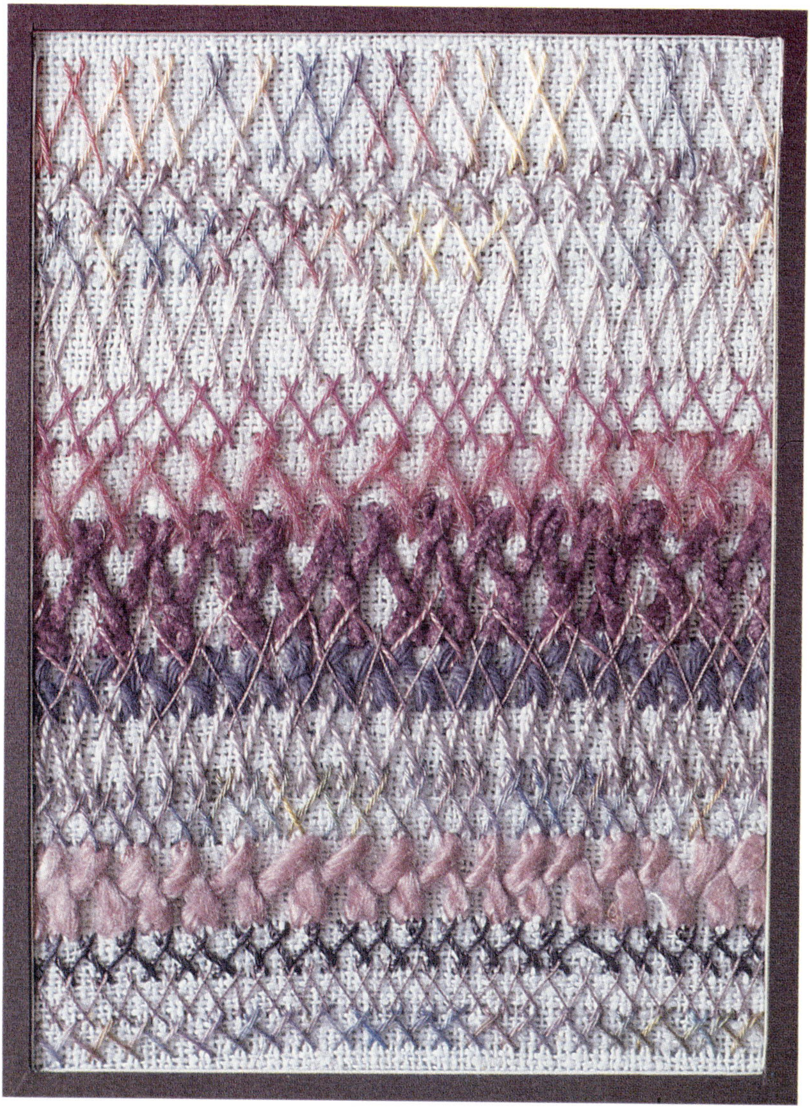

Herringbone stitch sampler A variety of threads has been used, from fine sewing silk to thick chenille and silk threads. The stitch has been worked quite traditionally, but each row varies in size and some of the rows overlap each other. Embroidered area: 4.5 x 6 inches (11 x 15 cm).

Materials & Techniques

Although the range of embroidery materials available these days is enormous, there is no need to buy everything at once. It is worth finding the address of the nearest specialist embroidery shop; most of these shops sell small quantities of fabrics, threads, etc, which cost very little and can be bought when required to add to the basic equipment.

Basic equipment: As well as threads and fabric, essential items are needles, scissors, pins, a thimble and a tambour embroidery frame. A range of needles will be required, including large-eyed ones such as chenille, to take thicker threads. Crewel embroidery needles are good general-purpose needles and come in a variety of sizes. As well as dressmaking scissors, small sharp-pointed embroidery scissors are a good investment. A medium-size tambour frame is useful for practising stitches and for embroidering small pieces of work. A square frame is useful for working larger pieces of work. Some embroiderers prefer to work without a frame but frames do help to prevent the work from distorting and make it easier to mount when finished.

Threads: The range is vast and often bewildering. If buying threads for the first time it is worthwhile keeping to a favourite colour scheme and buying a range of threads within that scheme, from fine machine embroidery threads to thicker knitting yarns, as well as silks and stranded cottons. Look for balls of interesting knitting yarn and crochet threads, and bear in mind suitability and thickness in relation to the work you intend to embroider. Other colours can be added when time and finances permit.

Fabrics: Once again, the choice is wide. Unbleached calico is cheap and provides an excellent fabric for practising stitches. It also makes a good background fabric for panels. It can also be used with fabric paints if colour is needed behind the stitchery. Plain polyester/cotton blends are also a good buy and will take fabric paints well. It is worth finding the specialist shop, where it is often possible to buy more expensive fabrics cut into small pieces. Silks are to be found in a mouth-watering selection of colours. Look out for sheer fabrics, organzas and lurex, leathers and suedes, all of which can be cut into tiny pieces and applied to the embroidery for special effects. Fabrics can be cut into narrow strips and used as thread themselves. Very delicate fabrics need a backing and may be best worked on a frame (see the section on using a frame).

Paints and dyes: Fabric paints are much in use these days to colour backgrounds for embroidery and these are available in most craft shops. There are many varieties on the market, but the beginner would probably be wise to buy some from an all-purpose range. These are usually fixed when dry by ironing on the reverse side. To begin with it is necessary to buy only the primary colours. They can be applied to the fabric with a cheap sponge or paintbrush and are great fun to experiment with. It is also possible to dye fabrics and threads in a microwave oven or washing machine. Suitable dyes are available in most department stores, together with a leaflet explaining how to use them. There are, of course, many other items to tempt the embroiderer, such as beads, sequins, narrow ribbons and metallic threads, and these can be added to one's range in time.

Design equipment: Most people will want at some time to design their own work and therefore some drawing equipment will be needed. This should include a small drawing pad, coloured pencils and lead pencils (B or 2B are preferable). Paints and brushes are useful but not everyone will want to invest in them straight away. A pad of tracing or greaseproof paper is also very useful, and a glue stick, ruler and scissors are essential.

Enlarging a design: Although it is possible to enlarge a design by drawing it out on an enlarged grid, the simplest method nowadays is to use a photocopier that has enlarging facilities. Copies should only cost a few pence and they save a great deal of time.

Transferring a design to fabric: There are several ways of doing this, the simplest being to place the fabric (if sufficiently transparent) over the drawing and trace directly onto it. There are water-soluble pens available for this purpose, but they should be used with great caution. Although in theory the lines can be washed away with cold water, they have an unfortunate habit of persisting in the fabric. The most foolproof method is probably by tracing and tacking. Make a tracing of the main outline of the design on greaseproof paper or tracing paper. Pin or tack this to the front of the background fabric and then carefully sew through all the lines with a good strong sewing cotton. When all the lines have been sewn down, the paper can be carefully torn away and the lines will be in place on the fabric ready to stitch over. These threads should be removed as the work progresses.

Using a frame: If the background fabric is particularly fine or difficult to handle, first stitch it on to a backing of calico or similar strong fabric. If using a tambour or ring frame the fabric should then be placed between the two rings and pulled as taut as possible without distorting the fabric.

Square frames: A square, or slate, embroidery frame consists of four strips of wood, two of which have canvas attached to them, to which the embroidery is sewn. The other two pieces slot into holes on the webbing bars, which can then be adjusted to the correct tension.

1. First mark the centre point of the strips of canvas and then mark the centre points of the top and bottom edges of your fabric.

2. Match up these centres and carefully sew the fabric to the two canvas strips.

3. Adjust the bars until the fabric is pulled taut.

4. Using a very strong thread oversew the sides of the fabric to the two side bars ensuring that the fabric is taut and unpuckered.

Finishing off: If a frame has been used, it should not be necessary to do anything to the work when it has been completed, but if a frame has not been used the work probably needs to be stretched. The best way to do this is as follows:

1. Cover a board with two or three layers of damp blotting paper.

2. Pin the work firmly in place, and with the embroidered surface upwards stretch it back into its correct shape.

3. Spray lightly with clean water and allow to dry thoroughly before removing.

Mounting a small panel: There are several ways to mount finished work, one of the simplest being to lace the embroidery over card before framing in a ready-made frame. You should choose a frame appropriate to the size of your work, probably including an area of unembroidered background fabric to give some space around it as a 'mount'.

1. Cut a piece of strong, firm card to the chosen size, making sure that all the sides are straight.

2. Place the embroidery face-down on a clean work-top and lay the card in position on top of it.

3. Fold the fabric round the edges of the board, and pin to the board, checking that the embroidery is centrally placed.

4. Using a long length of strong thread, lace the two sides together and then the top and bottom edges.

The embroidery is then ready to be slipped into the purchased frame.

MACHINE EMBROIDERY

It is not necessary to own an expensive machine with numerous automatic patterns. A simple, straight-stitch machine will be sufficient. As all machines vary it is essential to have the machine instruction leaflet to hand.

Equipment: A small ring frame is essential for machine embroidery as the work must be flat and tight. You will also need a large assortment of machine needles, as they will break or blunt very quickly. Some machines have a separate bobbin case. If this is so, it is a good idea to purchase an extra case and remove the tension spring. Have to hand a variety of machine embroidery threads, and small pieces of assorted fabrics. Unbleached calico is excellent for practising. It is also possible to buy water-soluble fabric. This is machined over and then the fabric dissolved away, leaving a lace-like embroidered design.

Preparation for sewing: The fabric should be absolutely taut in the frame.

1. Remove the presser foot. Some machines have an embroidery foot which is very useful.
2. Lower or cover the feed plate.
3. Thread the machine and load the bobbin.
4. Place the stretched ring under the needle so that it lies flat on the bed of the sewing machine.
5. Lower the presser foot lever. Wind the fly wheel manually until the lower thread is brought up to the surface.
6. Begin stitching, guiding the ring carefully with both hands.

It takes a little time to master free machining. Inevitably, the thread will snap and needles will break, but the results make it well worth the effort involved. It is also worth investing in a good machine embroidery book, such as *Machine Embroidery: Stitch Techniques* (see bibliography).

HOW BEST TO USE EMBROIDERY STITCHES

Before beginning either a traditional or a free piece of work, it is very important that you master the stitches you are going to use, or the result will disappoint you, as well as wasting your time and materials.

Collect together a variety of threads and small pieces of fabric and make a selection of different stitches. There is no need to work determinedly through all the stitches mentioned; pick out some that are pleasing, one or two more difficult stitches and especially some that are not in common use. Learn how to do each stitch correctly and traditionally first of all. Then try some of the other suggestions given with the instructions for each stitch. Work the stitch in a variety of threads – smooth and shiny threads, matt wools, etc. Try using narrow ribbons or fabric cut into strips threaded into a large-eyed needle. Incorporate beads into the stitchery if possible. Work the

Eastern Lights II *This hanging was worked entirely in transparent fabrics, and the inspiration for the design came from a study of old Log Cabin patchwork quilts. A piece of silk organza was painted with fabric paints and a variety of sheer fabrics was held in place with herringbone stitch and running stitch worked in a metallic machine embroidery thread. French knots in fine silk threads and tiny sequins have been added. Embroidered area: 9 x 11 inches (23 x 28 cm).*

stitch in different sizes; in different directions; overlap the stitches with those in another row or area. Keep all these samples, and with each one write down the name of the stitches you used. You will thus build up a useful 'catalogue' of stitches and effects, to which you can, and will, refer as you do more adventurous embroidery.

Designing for embroidery: Most embroiderers, if they have had no experience of drawing or painting since leaving school, will be appalled at the thought of taking up a pencil. However, it is perfectly possible to design with stitches, and it is worth experimenting with a small piece of embroidery, working directly into the fabric. Keep a collection of photographs and magazine cuttings of anything of interest that could possibly give a theme or inspiration for a piece of embroidery. This could be a landscape or a flower garden, buildings or geometric shapes. Keep photographs of textures too, such as sandy shores, rust or brickwork. Indicate colour schemes that could be adapted for embroidery. In a small sketch book make a few preliminary sketches, adding notes on scale, colour or any points of interest. Forget about beautiful, detailed drawings; this will be essentially personal reference information. Select a photograph or drawing that is particularly appealing and that could possibly be worked into stitchery. Trace off the main shapes and transfer them to fabric. Dampen the background and add a faint wash of fabric paints in the colours required. Allow the fabric to dry; iron on the reverse to set the paints and place the fabric in a ring frame ready to begin to stitch. Think about the embroidery; how is it best translated into stitchery? What are the most suitable stitches to use? Refer back to some of the stitch samples to see if any of your experiments will be suitable. Do not use too many stitches in one piece of work: it is perfectly possible to work the entire piece in one stitch only – straight stitch perhaps, or stem stitch, or one of the lesser known stitches. If the design is an overall pattern, perhaps the whole piece could be carried out in couched threads. Restrict the colour scheme – perhaps shades of one colour with a little bright contrast to 'lift' the embroidery. Having thought it through, made your designs and selections, you will be ready to start.

Arrowhead

Arrowhead is an extremely simple but very attractive stitch. Small, straight stitches are worked at somewhat less than right angles to each other to produce v-shapes. Arrowhead is most often used as a filling stitch and can be worked in simple straight rows or at random, making the stitches overlap each other as in the sample illustrated. Worked in this way the stitch suggests foliage and is very useful when interpreting gardens or flowers in embroidery.

Try a combination of threads, from very fine sewing cottons to thick silks and wools. Build up dense areas of stitchery by overlapping stitches. You can also use a fine contrast thread to suggest flowers or seed heads.

Bring the needle through to the front of the fabric at A. Insert the needle at B and bring out again at C ready to start the next stitch.

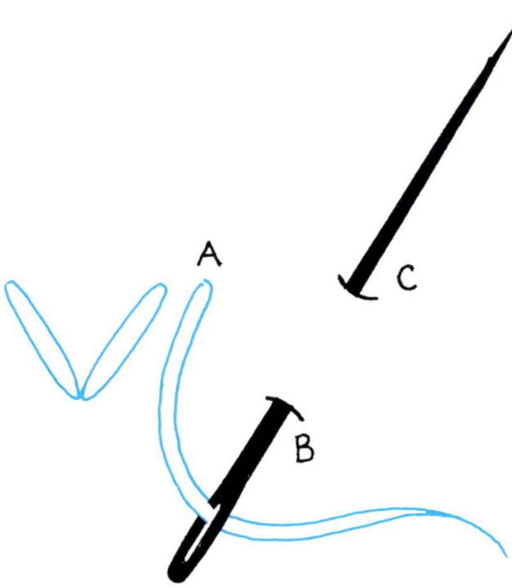

Back

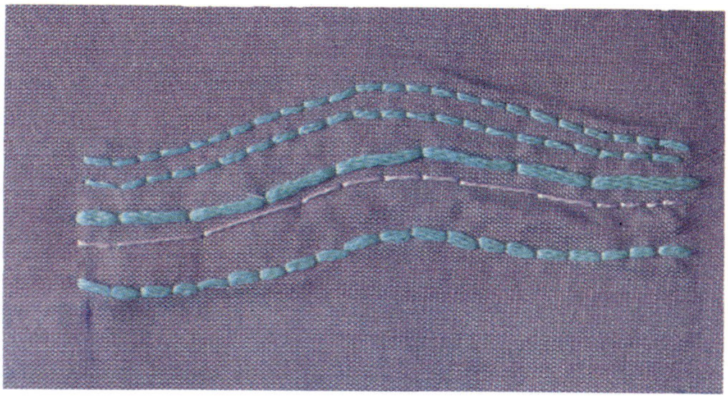

Back stitch appears as a continuous line of small stitches, simple to work but very effective. It is sometimes used as an outline stitch in counted thread work, and can also be used very effectively in quilting where tiny back stitches are worked in a thick thread.

Experiment with different threads and a variety of fabrics. It is not always necessary to work the stitch regularly and evenly. Combine tiny back stitches with long stitches – worked in a fine thread this is particularly useful in landscapes. Care should be taken, however, when using long stitches on certain embroideries that may require washing or will be exposed to constant wear – these stitches will catch and break quite quickly.

Bring the needle throughto the front of the fabric at A. Re-insert the needle at B, which should be immediately next to the last stitch. Bring the needle through to the front again at C, ready to commence the next stitch.

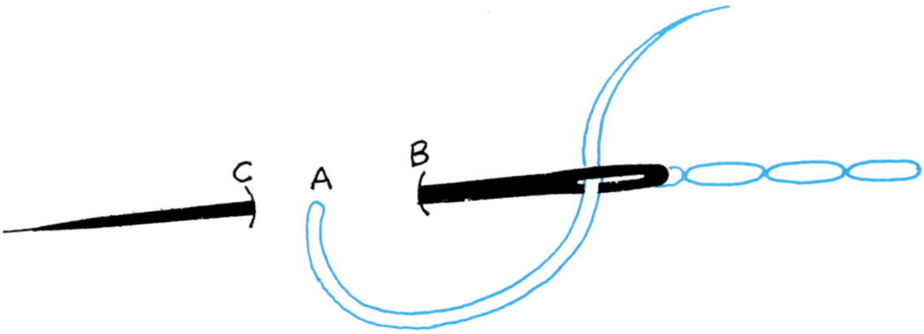

Threaded Back

This is a variation of back stitch. It produces a solid line of stitching and is particularly effective when two or more coloured threads are used.

Experiment with a variety of thicknesses of thread and combinations of threads within the one stitch. Try working the back stitch in differing lengths; this will result in rather an uneven stitch when it has been threaded with another silk but gives an interesting and unusual texture.

First, work a row of back stitch. Then, with a contrasting thread, take the needle under each stitch, changing direction each time. Apart from the beginning of the row and fastening off, the needle should not pierce the fabric at all. A second row of threaded stitches may then be worked, taking the needle through the opposite sides of the stitches, so that a chain effect is formed. This second row may be worked in another contrasting thread.

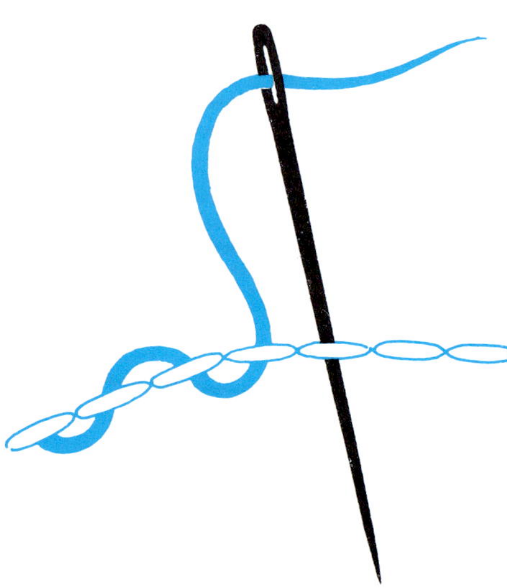

Basket

Basket stitch looks somewhat like herringbone stitch, although the working method is totally different. On the reverse of the fabric the stitches should appear as parallel vertical lines.

It is rather a wide, densely worked stitch and produces a heavy border which could be useful when building up a heavily textured surface. It is probably best worked in thicker threads and wools on a loosely woven fabric, as the finished effect is possibly too bulky for fine threads and fabrics.

Basket stitch is not quite as easy to work as other linear stitches and care should be taken to work the stitches in the correct sequence.

1. Bring the needle through to the front of the fabric at A and re-insert at B, above and a little to the right of A. Bring the needle out again at C on the same line as A.

2. Re-insert the needle at D, which is to the left of point B. Bring the needle out again at E, which is between points A and C.

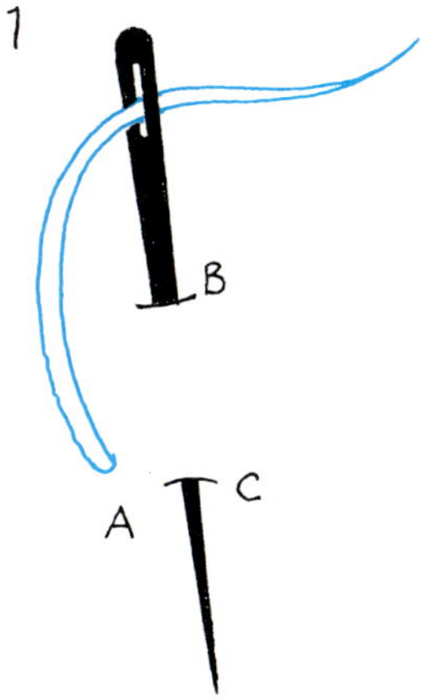

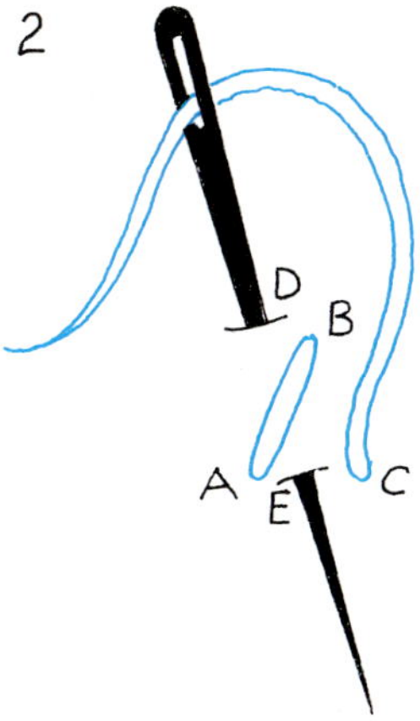

Basket Filling

Basket filling stitch forms an attractive, all-over pattern, which is equally effective on counted thread fabrics and on fine, tightly woven materials such as silk. Beware of using a fabric which has too uneven a weave, or is highly textured, as it will be quite difficult to work the stitch to produce a satisfactory effect.

Basket filling is particularly successful when a shiny, lustrous silk thread is used. Because the stitches are worked in different directions the light will catch the thread and different tonal effects will be achieved. Try working the stitch in one colour of thread on a contrasting coloured background. Different thicknesses of threads can be used. When using thicker threads, however, the individual stitches will be obscured as the threads will tend to merge into little blocks.

A block of four horizontal straight stitches should be placed beside a block of four vertical stitches in a chequerboard pattern, as in the diagram. Care should be taken to make the stitches as even and neat as possible (although, of course, absolute evenness will not be possible on a tightly woven fabric).

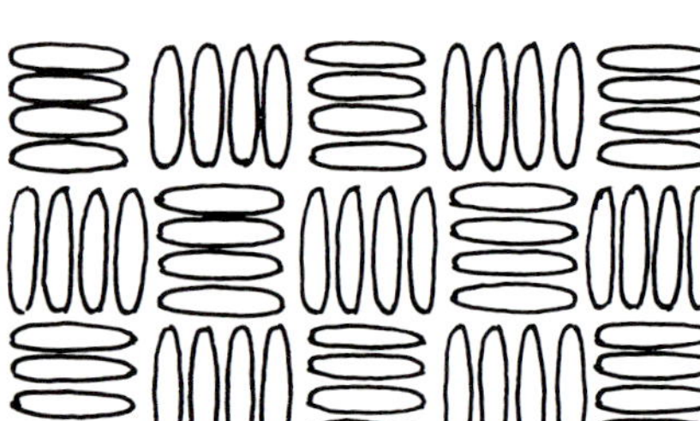

Brick

A quick, easy-to-work filling stitch. The manner of working is similar to long and short stitch, but it is not so finely stitched.

Smooth, medium-weight or slightly thicker threads are best; fine threads can be used, but it will take you longer to fill your fabric (brick stitch is often used to cover large areas of background fabric). It is possible to achieve shaded areas by working successive rows in toning threads. You can make the stitches quite large and irregular but care should be taken if they are used on something that gets a great deal of wear, as long stitches can easily snag.

For the first row only, bring the needle out to the surface at A. Insert again at B and bring out again at C, so that a short and then a long stitch is worked. In subsequent rows, stitches of equal size are placed in the spaces made by the row above.

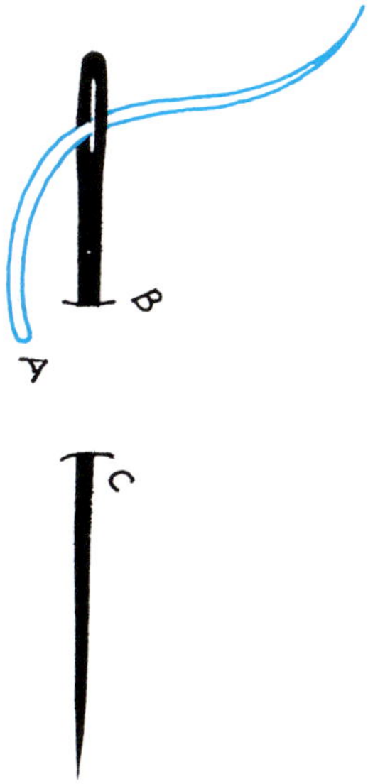

Brick and Cross Filling

Brick and cross filling is a pretty, all-over stitch, which can be used on counted thread fabrics as well as finer, tightly woven materials. Care should be taken when using an uneven weave fabric, or one that is textured, as it will be quite difficult to work the stitch effectively.

As in basket filling, brick and cross stitch is very effective when shiny, silky threads are used. Because the stitches are worked in different directions the light catches the thread and different tonal effects will be achieved. Try working the stitch in one-colour thread on a contrasting silk background. Contrasting coloured threads may be used, with the blocks worked in one colour and the crosses in another. Different thicknesses of thread can also be used.

Blocks of four horizontal straight stitches should be placed beside a small cross stitch (see under cross stitch for instructions). The arms of the crosses should all be worked in the same direction. Care should be taken to make the stitches as even and neat as possible, although absolute evenness will not be possible on a tightly woven fabric.

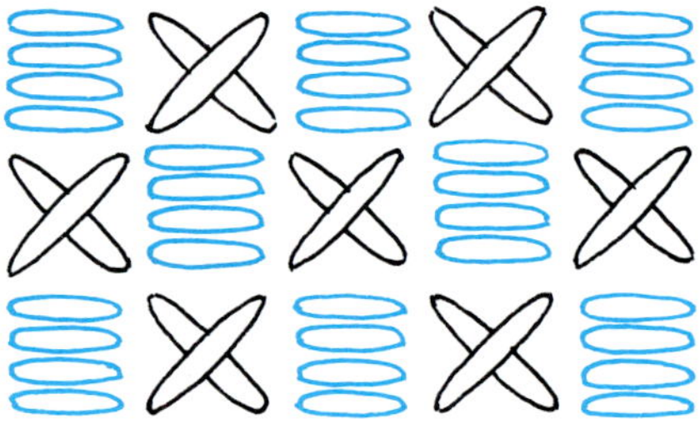

Bullion Knot

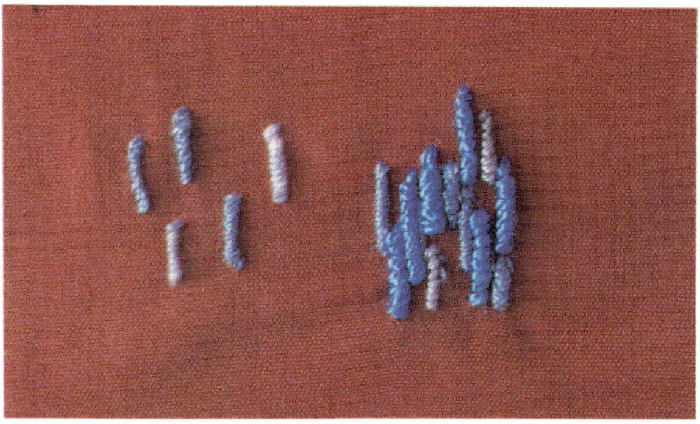

This stitch is sometimes referred to as caterpillar stitch. It is not an easy stitch to master and great care should be taken when working because the thread can easily become twisted and knotted. It is, however, a very versatile stitch and merits the time and effort needed to work it successfully. Practise first on a fabric such as calico or sheeting, preferably with a single untwisted thread. Most threads can be used, however, and it can be worked as an isolated, detached stitch, in rows to form interesting patterns, or grouped closely together in different types of threads, to portray foliage or seed heads.

Several bullion knots can be worked together, tightly packed upon themselves to produce tiny individual flowers – this stitch is often worked on lingerie or children's dresses.

Bring the needle out through the fabric at A, insert at B and bring it out again at A. Twist the working thread several times round the needle. Five or six times is probably enough, but this depends very much on the required size of the finished stitch. Then pull the needle very carefully through the fabric and the twisted thread. Re-insert the needle at B, pulling the working thread slightly and easing the twist into position.

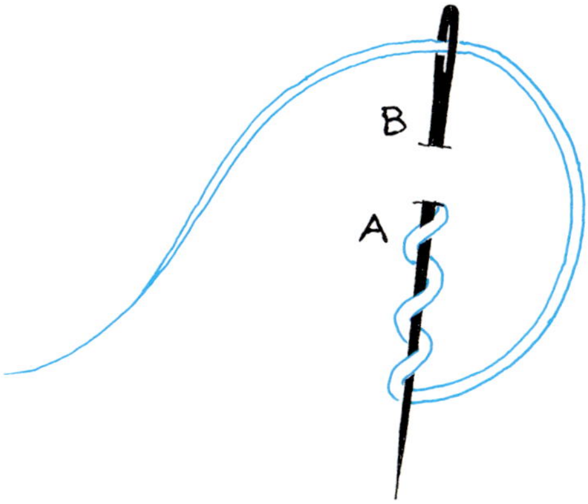

Burden

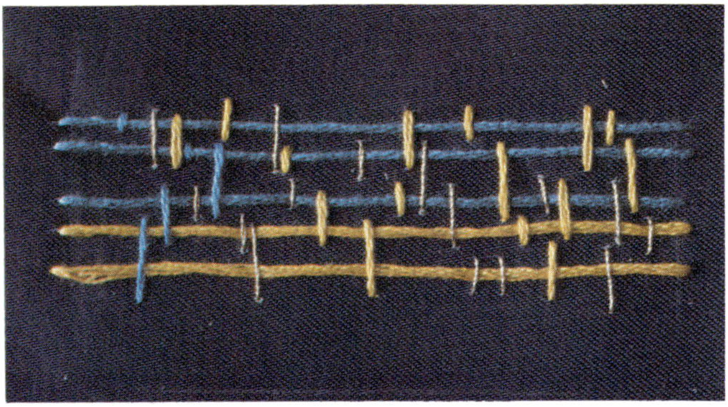

A form of couching often used in metal thread embroidery, burden stitch is quick to use and creates a very attractive pattern.

Traditionally, smooth threads were used for the couched lines but any thread can be used, from fine silks to thicker, more textured yarns. Gold purls are often used to hold down these threads, but any smooth thread can be used. The couched threads can be placed in a regular pattern, or spaced irregularly, and the couching stitches can be close together or wide apart. They can hold down just one thread at a time or several threads at once.

The couched threads are first laid down, then held in place by small, upright straight stitches.

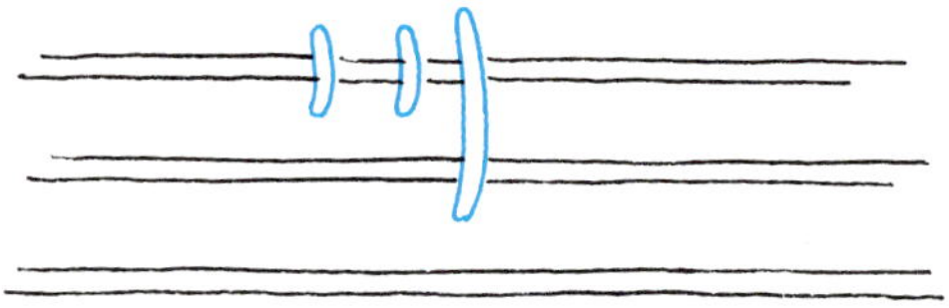

Buttonhole

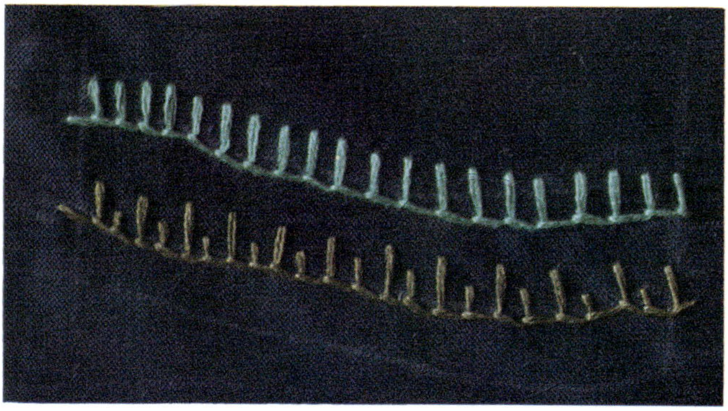

This is an infinitely variable stitch with many different forms and definitions. When spaced regularly it is often referred to as blanket stitch, probably because of its use as an edging on woollen blankets. When the stitches are worked closely together it produces a dense line of stitching. Experiment with different threads and thicknesses of thread. When worked regularly and evenly the finished result can be a little dull and uninteresting, but the lengths of each stitch can be varied, for instance, either regularly, as shown here, or at random, or the stitches could be spaced at irregular intervals. Many other interesting variations exist or can be devised by the inventive needleworker.

Bring the needle out through the fabric on the lower line. Re-insert it at A and bring it out again at point B, immediately below. The working thread should be placed underneath the needle, so that a loop is formed.

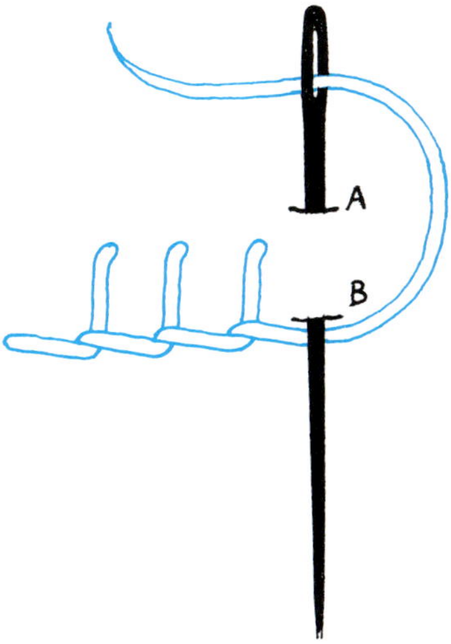

Buttonhole Filling

Buttonhole stitch can be used very successfully as a filling stitch, and in this form has several variations, of which the one illustrated is probably the simplest. It was often used in stumpwork embroidery and is also the basis of many needlepoint lace stitches.

First lightly mark on the fabric the outline of the shape to be worked. Experiment with all kinds of threads, from fine silks to thick wools. Use different-colour threads within the shape being worked, or a random dyed thread. Variations of the stitch can be worked by changing the spacing of the stitches, or working several stitches into one space.

The design can be made more three-dimensional by sewing down a padded layer of toning felt.

1. *Work a row of small loosely looped stitches across the top of the shape.*

2. *On the next row, work a row of buttonhole stitches, taking the needle through each of the loops on the row above. The needle does not pierce the fabric except at the beginning and end of each row. On the following rows the needle is taken through the loop of the stitch above.*

1

2

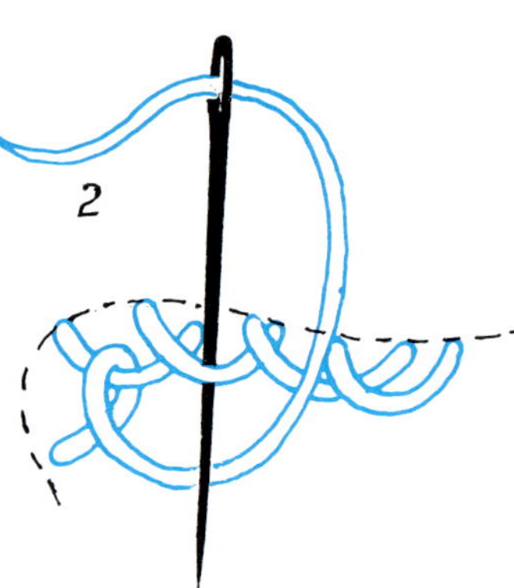

Detached Buttonhole

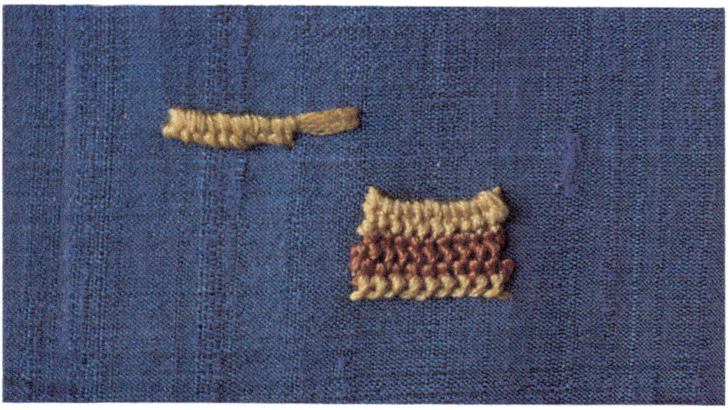

This is not difficult to work but as it is so tightly stitched it is necessary to work to an even tension. Practise on a spare piece of fabric until you are satisfied with the result. Experiment with a variety of threads, but you will find that thick threads will be quite difficult to work. Use different-colour threads or a random dyed thread.

As with buttonhole filling stitch, it is important first to mark the outline of the shape to be worked on the fabric. The shape can be raised by sewing down a padded layer of felt before stitching, using felt of the same colour as the working thread.

1. With the working thread, sew two long stitches right across the shape.

2. Then work a row of buttonhole stitches, taking the needle over the long stitches, working the stitches as closely together as possible. The needle does not enter the fabric except at the beginning and end of each row. On the following rows the needle is taken through the loops of the stitches of the row above.

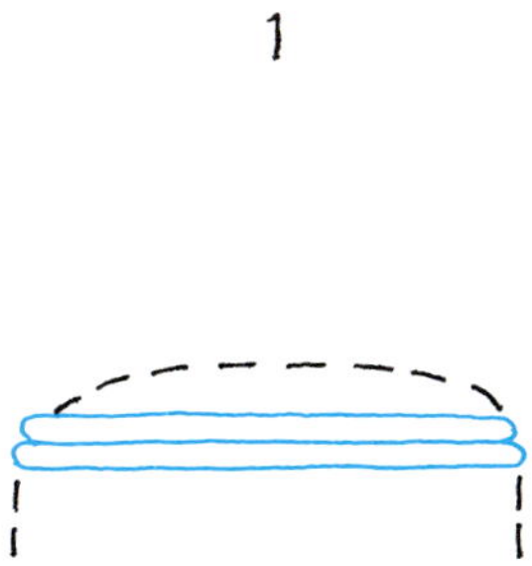

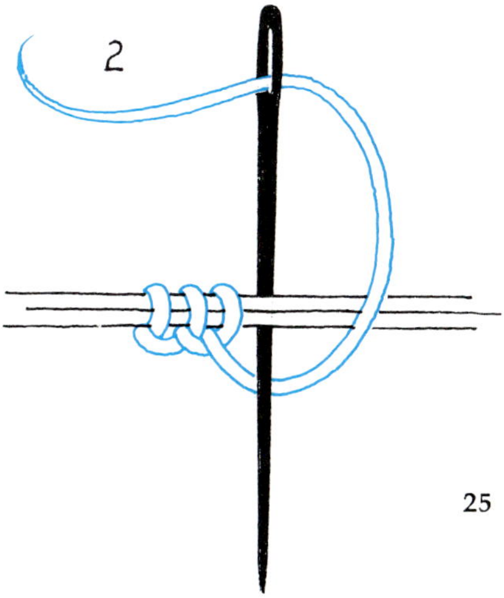

isolated *Buttonhole Stitch Wheel*

This is another variation of buttonhole stitch, but used here as an isolated stitch. It is quite simple to work but care should be taken to stitch the circle as neatly and evenly as possible, although it is not always easy to be absolutely exact.

The stitch can be used very successfully for flower heads when embroidering gardens and landscapes. Use different thicknesses of thread, although it is probably easier to work in fine silks and cottons than thick wools. Try overlapping the wheels to achieve a rich, textured surface.

It is advisable to mark the circle on the fabric before starting to stitch, as it is quite difficult to achieve a circle without any guidelines.

Work buttonhole stitches around the shape with the looped edge on the outside. The stitches should be quite close together but they will, of course, be much closer at the centre than on the outer edge.

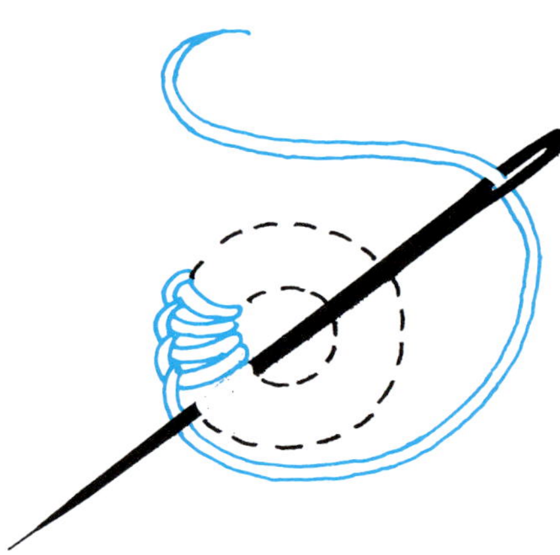

Cable

This attractive linear stitch is not particularly difficult to use, but it does require some practice. It forms quite a thick border stitch and is very attractive if used as an edging on a garment. Instead of being worked on a straight or curved line the stitches can be worked at an angle of 45° to each other, as illustrated.

Try a variety of thicknesses of threads. If thick yarns and silks are used, and the lines of stitches are worked close together, a very interesting texture can be achieved. Finer threads and metallic threads could be stitched over them.

Hold the working thread down on the fabric with the left hand. Then twist the thread round the needle as shown in the diagram. Insert the needle through the fabric at A and bring up to the surface at B, with the working thread lying under the point of the needle. It is very important that the thread is twisted in the correct way or the stitch will not be formed. When working on the next stitch the needle will be inserted very close to B.

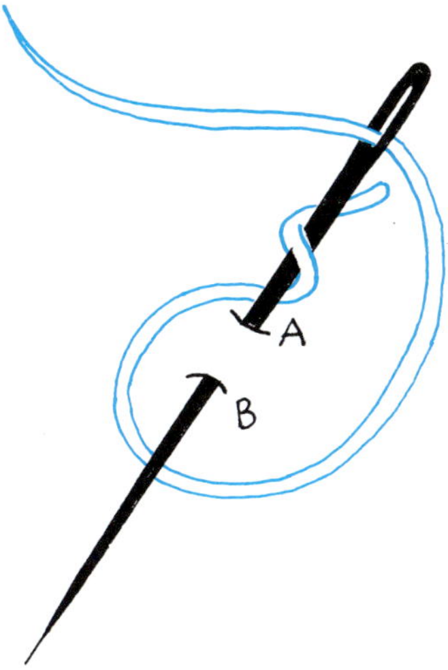

Chain

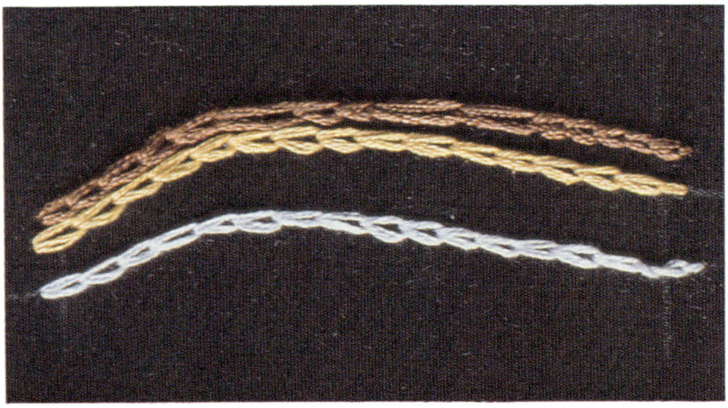

Chain stitch is basically a linear stitch but as there are so many variations I have grouped them together in their own category. Some of the variations are included here but there are many more.

Chain stitch can be worked in almost any type of thread, from fine sewing cotton and machine metallic threads to thick wools. It is extremely useful for creating patterns, textures or just a simple row of stitches, perhaps when working a landscape. Try varying the size of each stitch, making some quite long; work the rows of stitches very close together so that they form a thick texture. Further rows could be worked over the top, perhaps in a different direction to give added interest.

Bring the needle out to the surface of the fabric and insert it at A. Bring it out again at B with the thread looped underneath the point of the needle, as in the diagram. To work the next stitch the needle will again be inserted into the fabric at B, and out at C.

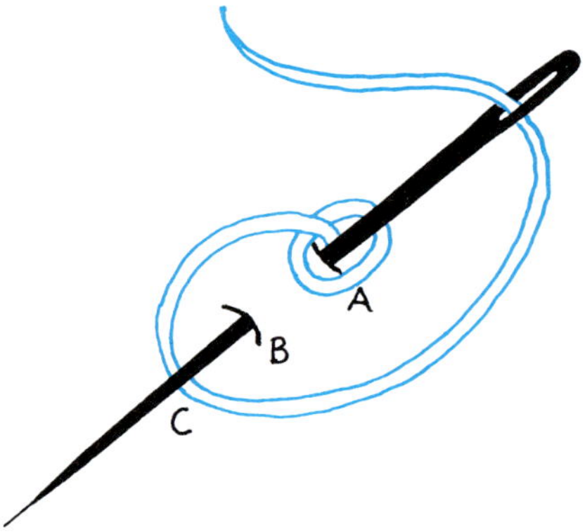

Detached Chain

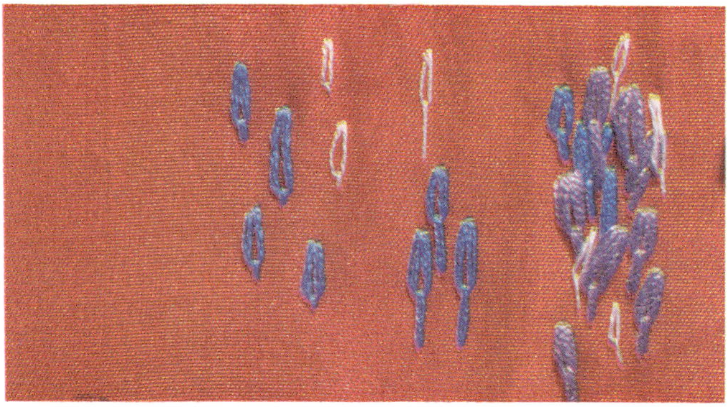

This very useful stitch, also known as lazy daisy, forms convincing flowers and seeds and can also be used to build up foliage when depicting gardens or landscapes. As an isolated stitch it forms flower heads, and massed together it forms textures and patterns. Try a variety of threads from very fine sewing cottons to thick wools and yarns. To build up textured areas, work the stitches in different sizes and on top of each other in an assortment of threads of all thicknesses. For added interest the 'tail' or 'stalk' of the stitch can be made much longer than usual.

1. Bring the needle out to the front of the fabric at A. Then re-insert the needle at exactly the same spot and bring it out again at B, with the thread lying under the needle.
2. Re-insert the needle at C and bring out again at D ready to work the next stitch.

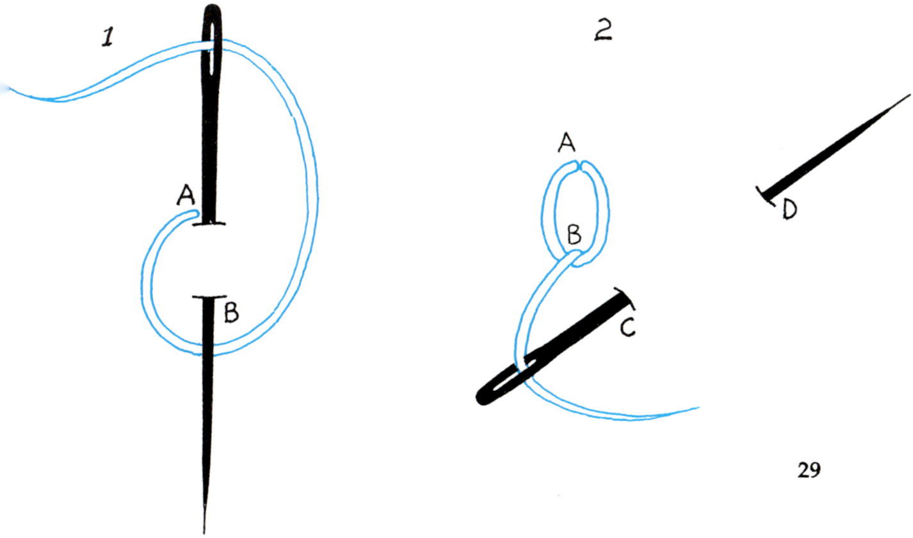

Feathered Chain

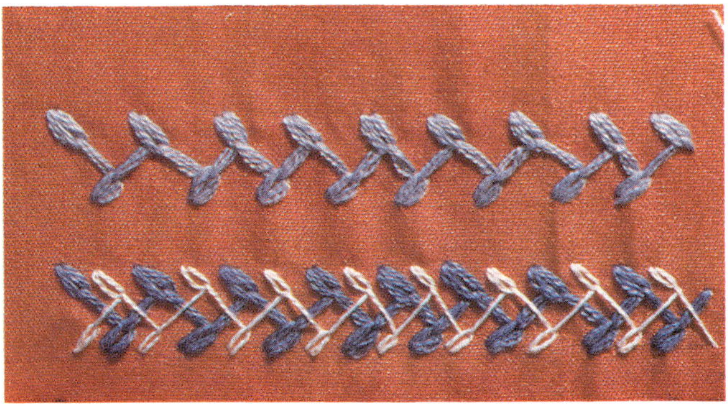

This stitch forms an attractive, quite wide, border stitch. Although it looks complicated, it is simple to work, but care should be taken to keep the stitches as regular and as even as possible or the overall charm of the stitch will be lost. To help achieve this it is a good idea to mark two parallel rows on the fabric before beginning.

Feathered chain stitch is very useful when working patterns of stitchery, or as a border to surround a piece of freely worked stitchery. It is a formal stitch and although it *could* be worked quite freely it then tends to lose its attractiveness. The stitches can be worked closely together or spaced further apart. A second, and even a third line of stitchery could be worked over the top in contrasting colours, as in the sample above, or in a metallic thread.

1. Bring the needle out of the fabric at A. Re-insert at the same spot and bring out again at B with the thread lying under the needle, thus forming a chain stitch.

2. Insert the needle into the fabric at C and bring out again at D, ready to work another chain stitch.

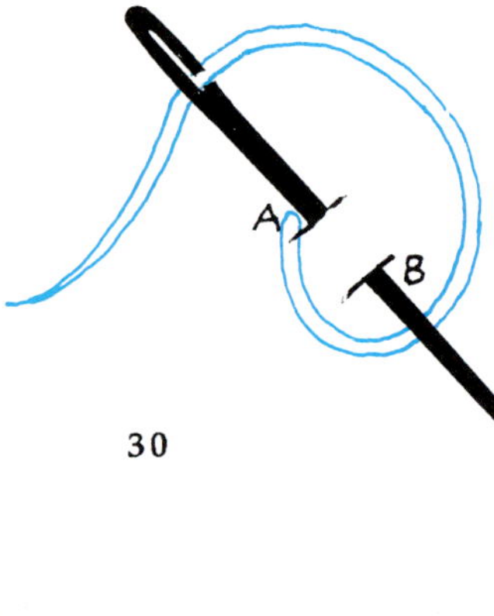

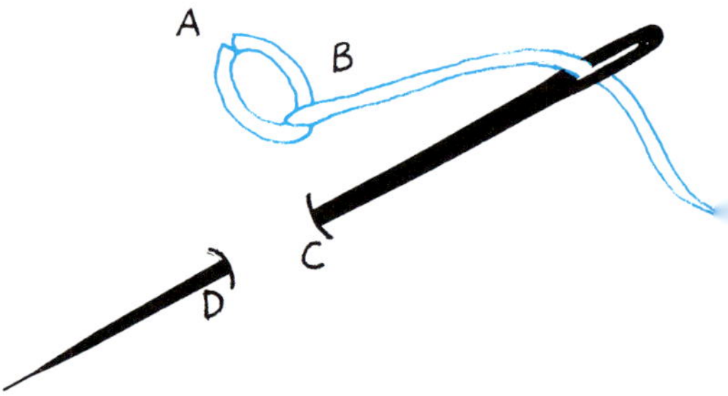

Knotted Chain

This is a variation of chain stitch which requires a little care to work, as the correct tension is important and quite difficult to achieve, though it will come with practice. It is, however, an effective border stitch and looks especially good when worked in thick, shiny threads, wools or metallic yarns. It can be very useful when creating surface textures, or as a row of textured stitches when working a landscape. Experiment by working the rows of stitches close together so that they form a thick overall pattern.

1. *Working from right to left, bring the needle out to the surface of the fabric at A. Insert at B and bring out again at C, forming a small, diagonal stitch.*

2. *Slip the needle through this stitch, without piercing the fabric.*

3. *Again without piercing the fabric, slip the needle through the loop formed. Pull the needle carefully through the thread so that the knot lies on the fabric to the left of the stitch.*

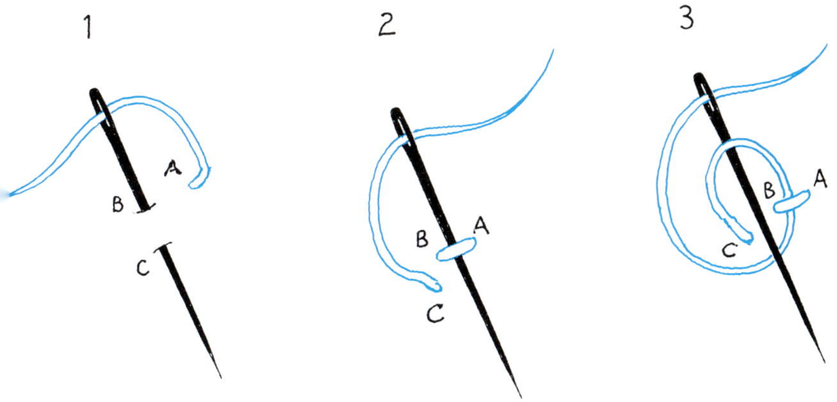

Open Chain

This is a very broad stitch and should be worked with care as it can look quite ugly. It is, however, a versatile stitch and useful if different textures and surface interest are required. It is better worked in medium-weight to thick yarns. By inserting the needle into the fabric almost horizontally, the widths of the stitch can be altered greatly. Try working the rows so that they lie very close to each other and then experiment by working further rows on top of them.

Bring the needle out to the surface of the fabric and insert it at A. Bring it out again at B with the thread looped underneath the point of the needle, as in the diagram. The loop should be held quite loosely or it will be difficult to complete the stitch. To work the next stitch, the needle will again be inserted into the fabric below A. The size of the stitch can be altered by varying the angle that the needle is inserted into the fabric.

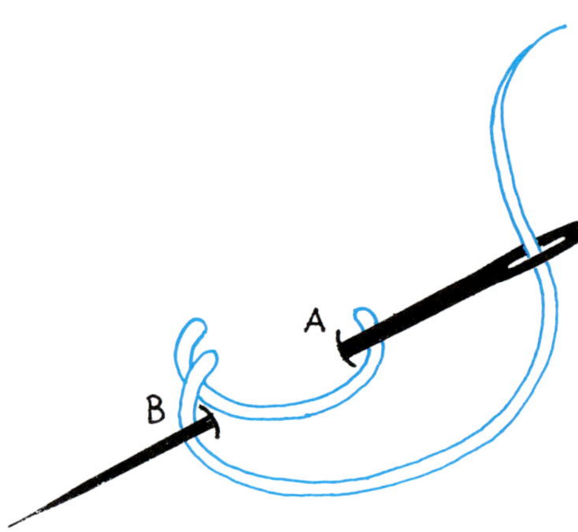

Raised Chain Band

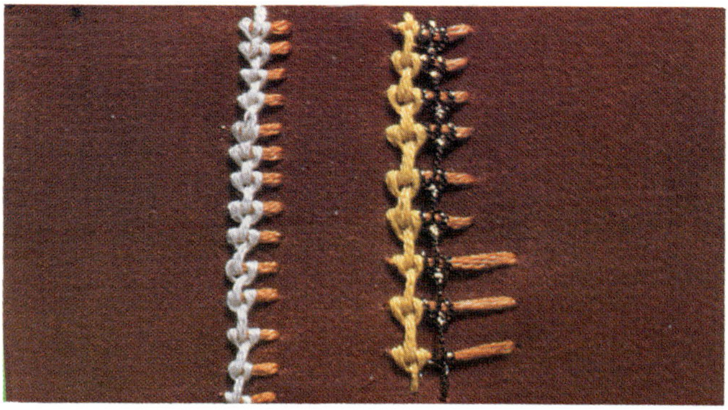

This is a form of chain stitch worked on a row of horizontal stitches. It is very attractive, extremely versatile and fairly simple to work. Experiment with all types and thicknesses of threads. It is not necessary for the horizontal stitches to be the same colour or type as the chain stitches. Varying the distance between the horizontal stitches will result in an uneven and interesting stitch. Work the stitches close together so that an overall texture is formed. Make the horizontal stitches quite wide so that several chain stitches can be worked together. Add metallic threads and ribbons.

1. *Work a row of horizontal stitches.*

2. *Bring the needle out through the fabric at A and loop underneath the horizontal stitch at B without piercing the fabric. Take the needle underneath the horizontal stitch at C with the thread looped under the point of the needle, and again without entering the fabric.*

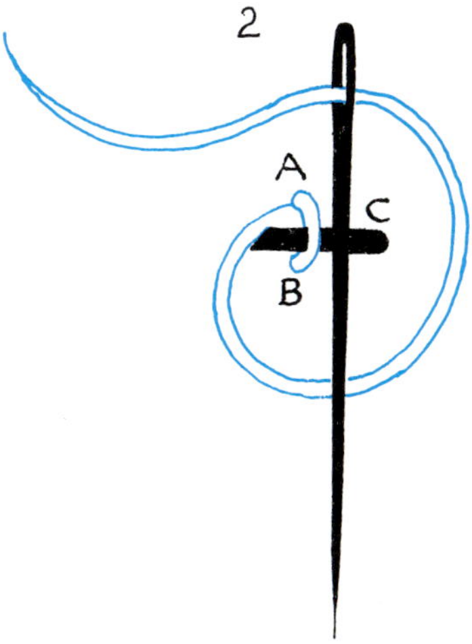

Rosette Chain

This is sometimes known as bead edging stitch, and does indeed give the appearance of a row of tiny beads. It requires some practice and is best worked in a medium-weight thread, although this choice will, of course, depend on the nature of the work. It makes an attractive border stitch and would be useful as an edging on a garment. Try using bright silks and cotton threads.

1. Work from right to left. Bring the needle out at A. Insert the needle at B and bring out again at C, with the thread looped over the needle as shown in the diagram. Pull the needle carefully through the fabric, being careful not to pull the thread too tightly.

2. Slip the needle under the stitch at D. The needle should not pierce the fabric. The next stitch is now ready to be worked.

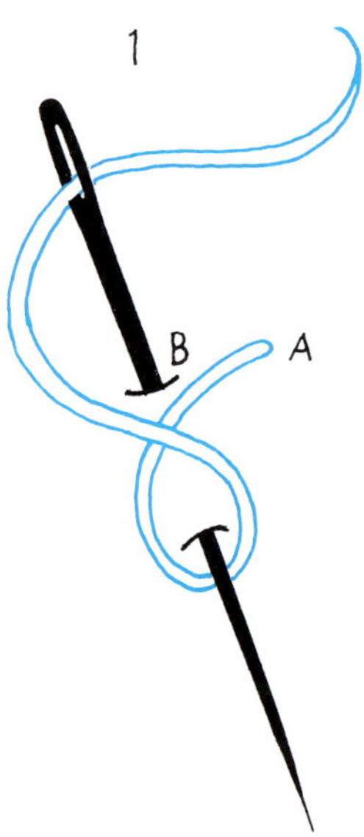

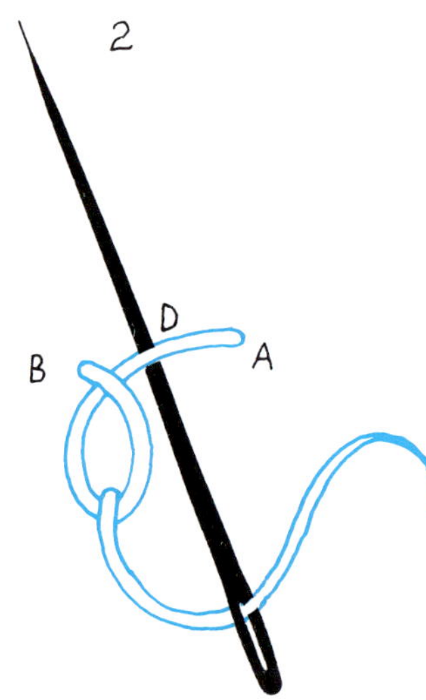

Twisted Chain

A variation of simple chain stitch, this forms a raised line of stitches, useful for borders and patterns. It is not particularly difficult to work, although care should be taken to achieve a good tension and it is probably best worked in medium-weight threads. However, it is interesting worked in thicker threads and on a fairly coarse background fabric. It also looks particularly well when metallic threads are used. Try varying the length of the stitch within the line from fairly long to very close together. Build up texture by working the stitch so that each line encroaches on the next. Other rows could be worked on top, at an angle to those already worked.

Bring the needle out to the front of the fabric at A. Insert the needle at B and bring out again at C with the thread passing first over and then under the needle.

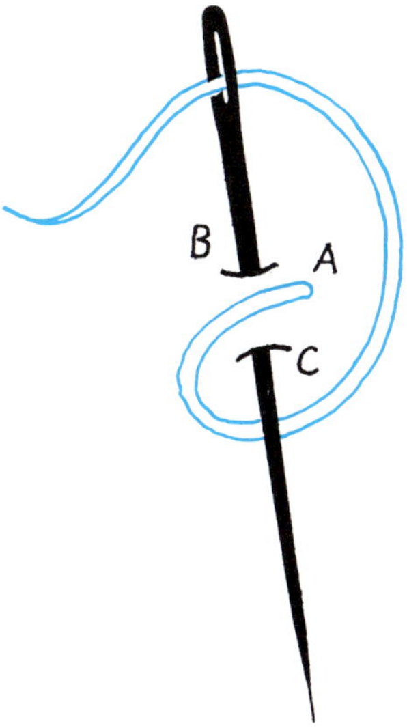

Whipped Chain

This is a version of simple chain stitch in which a second thread is added to the line of stitchery after it has been worked. The stitch formed is raised and solid and would be useful where added texture is required. The whipped thread can be the same colour as the line of stitchery, or a contrasting or toning colour. Experiment with an assortment of threads, including metallic and textured knitting yarns. A second whipped thread can be added, perhaps in a contrasting colour. Lines of stitches can be packed closely together to make interesting patterns, and if the threads vary in thickness, secondary textural patterns will be formed. Use whipped chain stitch next to other chain stitches and linear stitches. To build up areas of texture, work the stitch so that each line encroaches on the next. Other rows could be worked on top, at an angle to those already worked.

Work a line of chain stitches (see chain stitch for working instructions). Then, working from right to left, take the needle beneath each stitch without piercing the background fabric. Do not pull the thread or the row of stitches will become distorted.

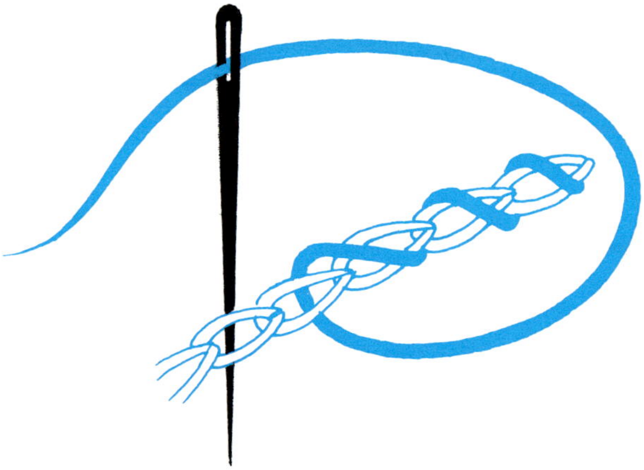

Chevron

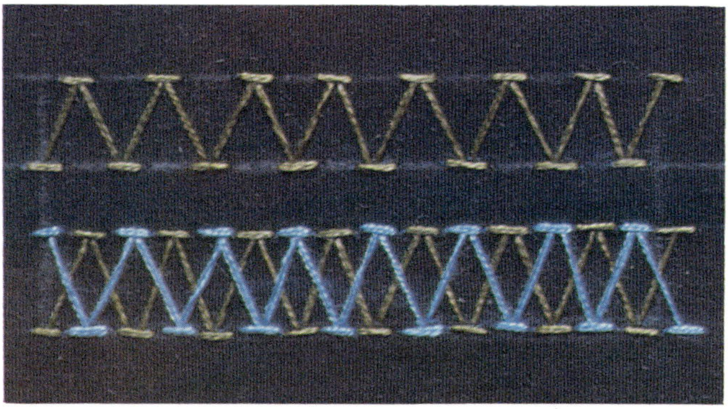

Chevron stitch is a wide border stitch, simple to work and rather similar in appearance to herringbone stitch. It is useful when working formal patterns rather than in free embroidery. Experiment with threads in a wide variety of thicknesses. The stitches can be worked quite close together or spaced far apart. Try varying the width of the stitches to obtain a freer effect. A second, and possibly a third line of stitchery can be worked over the top in contrasting colours or metallic threads. To build up a pattern, work rows of chevron stitch so that each subsequent row encroaches on the first. To keep the stitch even, it is a good idea to lightly mark two parallel lines, on which the short bar stitches will lie, on the fabric before beginning.

1. Bring the needle out through to the front of the fabric at A. Insert the needle at B and bring out again at C.
2. Re-insert the needle at D and bring out again at E. Note that point E is at the same spot as point B.

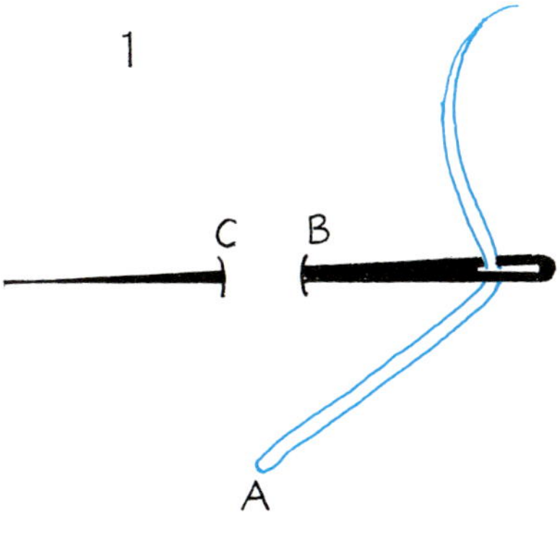

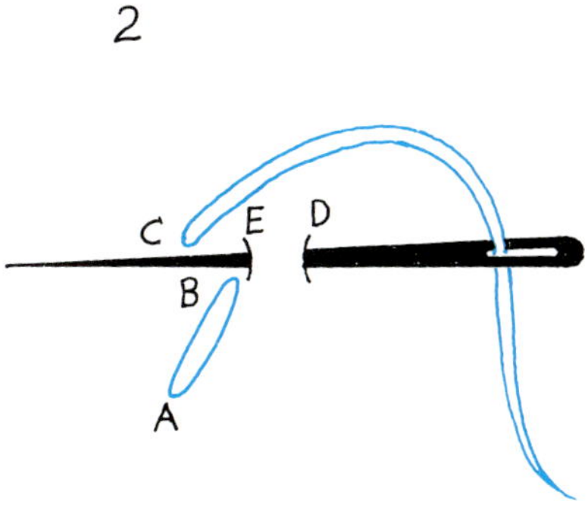

Cloud Filling

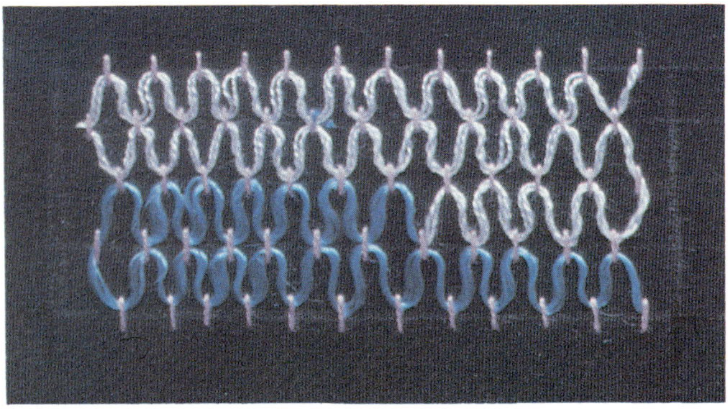

This is a charming and attractive filling stitch which is simple to work. Cloud stitch is worked on a base of small vertical stitches, and a second thread is then threaded through them to form a pattern. Fine to medium-weight threads are best, as otherwise some of the delicate nature of the stitch will be lost. Bright silks or random dyed threads are particularly attractive. The scale of the pattern can be varied by alternating the arrangement of the vertical stitches, setting some close together and others far apart. It is a good stitch to use for an area of plain fabric where some sort of texture is called for, the thread matching or toning with the background fabric.

1. *Work a grid of small vertical stitches. These stitches should be arranged in a half drop repeat pattern.*

2. *With a contrasting thread, take the needle through each stitch in turn. Note that this thread should not pierce the background fabric.*

1

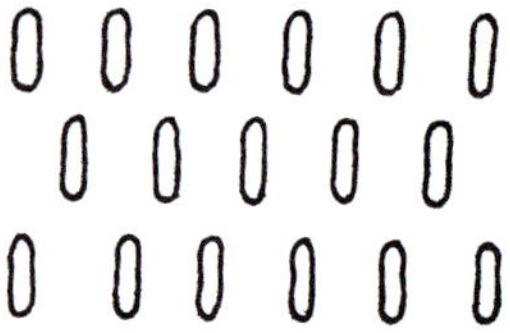

2

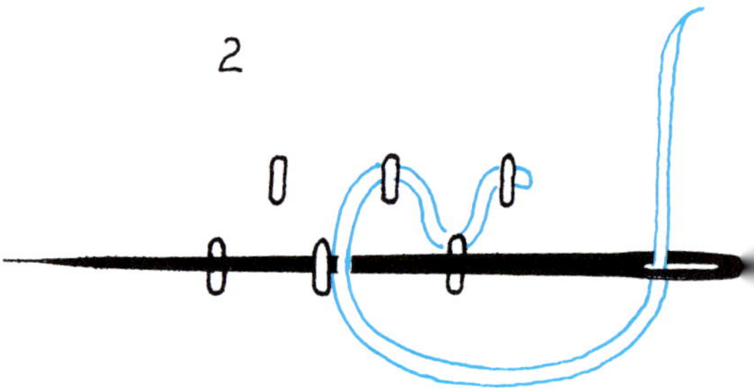

Coral

This is a fine linear stitch, easy to work, and forming an attractive textured border stitch. It is particularly useful when working landscapes or foliage, and can look very interesting if used in conjunction with, for example, smooth stitches such as chain or running stitch. It can be worked in any thread, from fine to thick knitting yarns, and also looks well in metallic threads. Experiment with the lines of stitchery, working some of the 'knots' close together and some much further apart, so that the stitch appears stretched. To build up areas of texture, work it so that each line encroaches on the next. Other rows can be worked on top, at an angle to those already worked.

Bring the needle out to the front of the fabric at A. Insert the needle at B and bring out again at C, with the thread lying over and then under the needle.

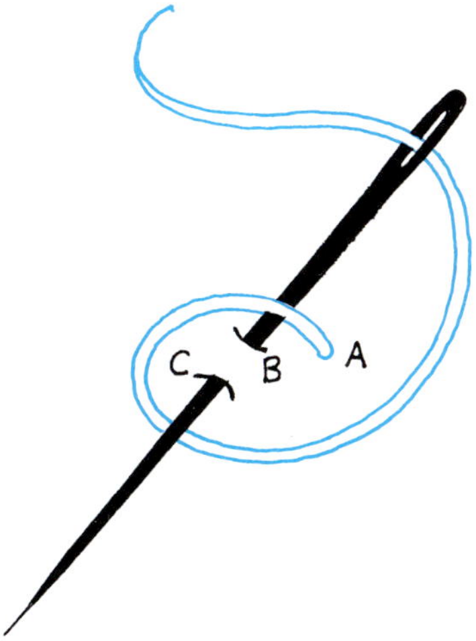

Couching

A very simple and extremely versatile stitch, consisting of rows of threads held down with tiny stitches placed at right angles to the row and usually at regular, even intervals. One of the many forms of couching is used in metal thread embroidery, when imitation Japanese gold and other metallic threads are held down with a fine silk thread, as illustrated in the sample above. Although the stitching thread should be fairly fine, the couched threads can consist of anything from fine and medium-weight embroidery threads to textured weaving yarns. Several threads can be held down at a time and these can be varied in texture and colour. For more interest the stitching thread can be varied – spaced much closer together at some intervals than at others, and this thread could be of a bright contrasting colour. Although the most common stitch is a tiny 'vertical' stitch, you could experiment with other tying-down stitches, such as cross stitch, detached chain, or Cretan stitch.

Place the thread to be couched across the fabric (it is often helpful to anchor it with pins). Insert the needle into the fabric at A and bring out again at B.

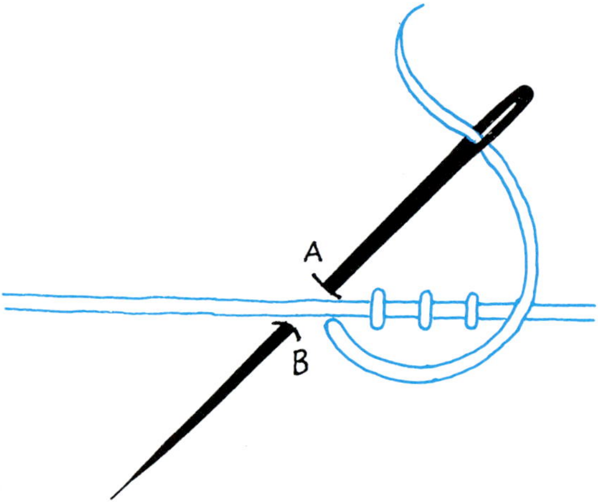

Indian Purse The design for this piece of embroidery was taken from a fragmant of Indian embroidery. Lurex, sheer fabric and coloured papers were applied to a silk background fabric. Imitation Japanese gold thread and stranded cottons were couched down with coloured silk threads. Seeding stitch has been worked in some parts of the design. Embroidered area: 4.5 x 4.5 inches (11 x 11 cm).

Battlement couching sampler *A piece of space dyed silk organza was applied to a silk background fabric. The couched threads are a mixture of silk and cotton, held in place with cross stitches worked in silk, cotton and metallic threads. Running stitch was used as a frame. Embroidered area: 4 x 7 inches (10 x 17.5 cm).*

Battlement Couching

Although more complicated than some of the other couched filling patterns, battlement couching is, nevertheless, quite quick to work when large ares of background have to be covered. A little care needs to be taken to ensure that the tension is correct. Smooth, fine or medium-weight threads should be used. As several different threads are used to build up the pattern, exciting colour combinations can be achieved by using contrasting threads. Traditionally, the threads are laid down at regular intervals. However, interesting results can be obtained by working an irregular grid, as shown above.

1. With the first colour, lay down long horizontal threads. These are then covered with rows of vertical threads in the same colour.

2. With the second colour, lay horizontal threads just above the first row of threads. The vertical threads should then lie just to the right of the first colour. This is repeated with the third and fourth colour threads. When the grid has been completed, the last row of threads is tied down at each intersection with a small diagonal stitch (see photograph above).

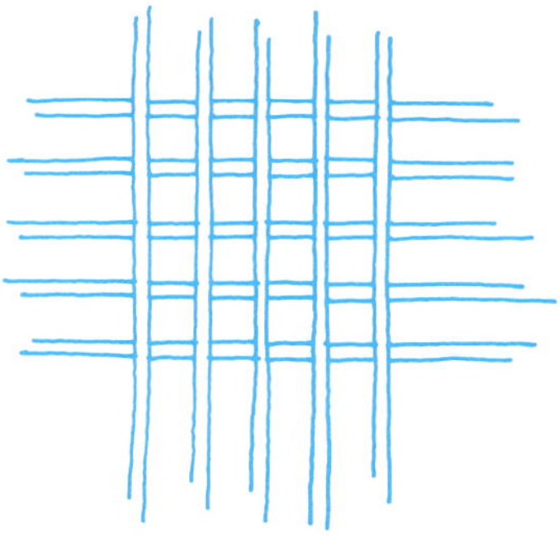

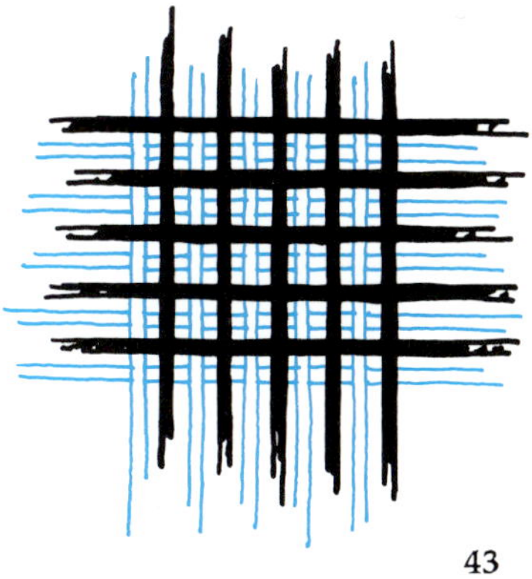

Bokhara Couching

Bokhara couching is an effective filling stitch, although it can equally well be used as a linear stitch. It differs from ordinary couching in that the same thread is used for the couched thread as for the tying down. The working method is similar to Roumanian couching although the finished effect is somewhat different. The opportunities for experiment are a little limited, but the effect of this stitch can vary dramatically according to the threads used. With thick floss silk or stranded embroidery threads a shiny lustrous surface will be produced; with a twisted thread the result will be slightly raised and textured, and an interesting effect will also be achieved if the whole area is worked with a random dyed thread.

1. Start at the edge of the shape to be covered. Bring the needle out to the surface of the fabric at A. Re-insert at B, diagonally opposite A, also on the edge of the area to be covered. Bring the needle out again at C.

2. Re-insert at D. Bring the needle out again at E. The tying down thread should lie diagonally across the couched thread.

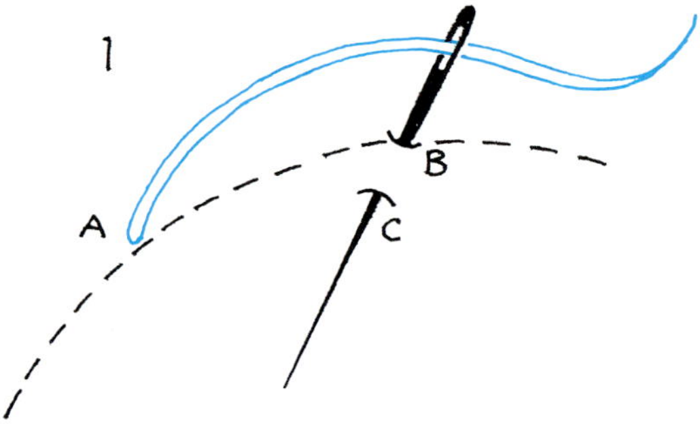

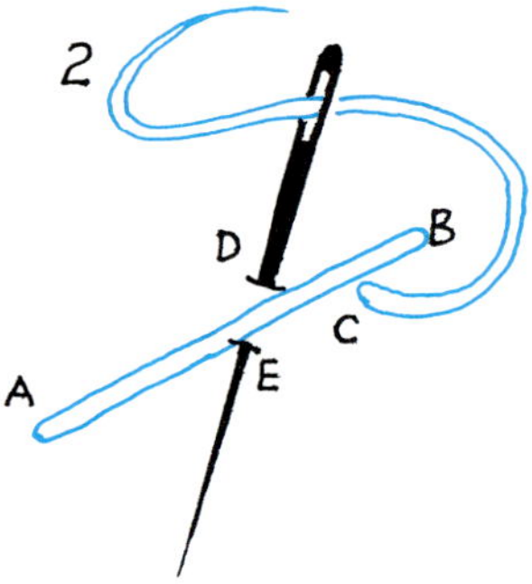

Couched Filling

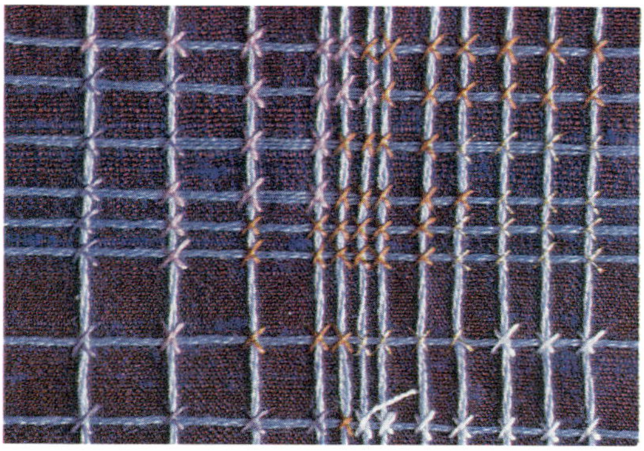

This is an attractive filling stitch, very simple to work, and producing interesting surface patterns. Rows of horizontal and vertical lines are placed across the fabric and held in place with small cross stitches. The threads are usually laid down in regular intervals, but far more interesting results can be obtained when an irregular grid is made. Any thread or combination of threads can be used for the grid pattern. The cross stitches are usually quite small, but try varying the size of these and also the colours of the thread. Metallic threads look very effective. Other stitches, or beads or sequins, could be placed in the spaces in the grid.

First, lay the horizontal threads. It is important to keep a good tension. If the threads are too tight, the fabric will pucker and if they are too loose, they will not form an even surface pattern. The vertical threads can then be placed in position. Both vertical and horizontal threads are only taken through the fabric at the beginning and end of each row. At each intersection of the threads, a small cross stitch is made, usually in a contrasting thread.

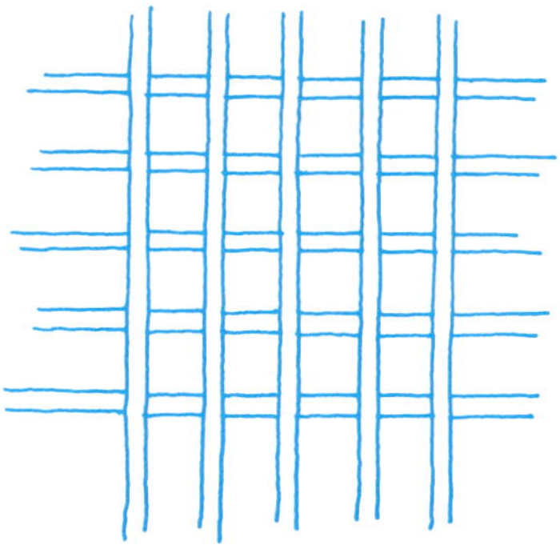

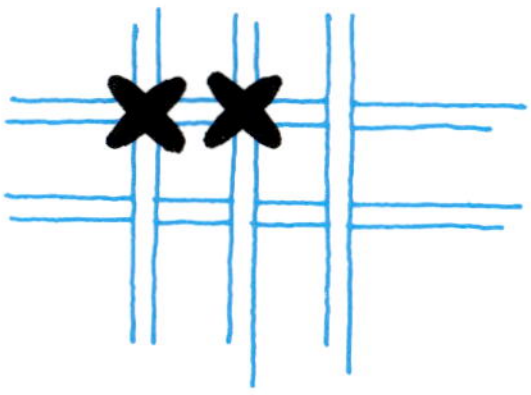

Pendant Couching

A little care is needed to work this variation of couching. As the couched thread is looped, it is not very suitable for anything that is going to wear, such as garments or cushions.

The main interest in this stitch is in the threads that are couched down and it is therefore better to keep the stitching thread fine. However, it looks particularly attractive when contrasting threads are used. The couched threads can be anything from fine and medium-weight embroidery threads to textured knitting yarns. Several threads can be held down at a time and these can be varied in texture and colour. Pendant couching is particularly successful when strands of fine metallic threads are used.

As in couching, the threads are held down with tiny vertical stitches, usually worked in pairs, the couched thread being formed into a loop between each pair of stitches. Try to keep the loops all the same size if possible.

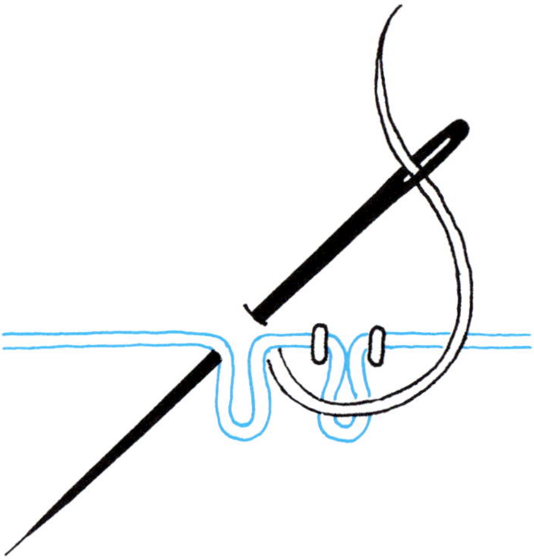

Roumanian Couching

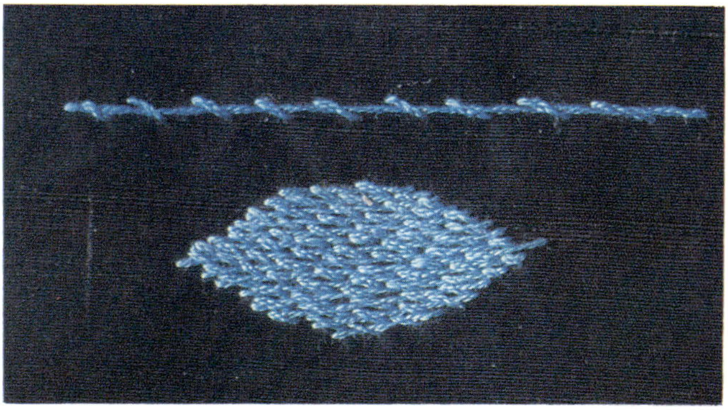

This is similar to Bokhara couching, although the finished effect is different. It is not difficult to work but care needs to be taken to obtain the correct tension. The same thread is used for the couching and tying down. Roumanian couching is generally used to fill large shapes. Its use as an experimental stitch is limited but interesting results can be achieved by varying the colour or thickness of threads. A random dyed silk would look attractive. Smooth, medium-weight threads are easiest to use.

1. Bring the needle out at A and insert at B, which is at the opposite side of the shape to be covered.
2. Bring the needle out at C. Insert at D and bring out again at E, ready to commence the next stitch. These tying-down stitches are quite long and should not be pulled too tightly.

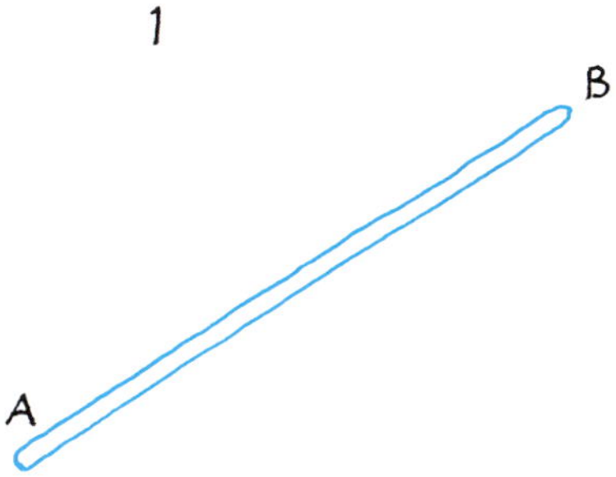

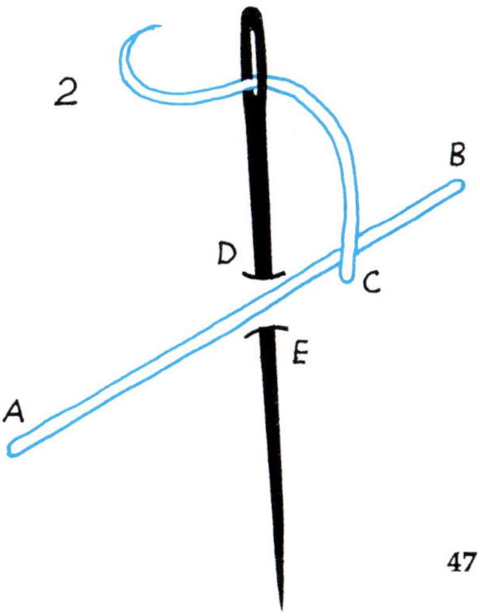

Trellis Couching

This is a useful stitch for filling large areas of background fabric. It is not a difficult stitch but care should be taken to ensure that the threads are laid down at an even tension. Because of the diagonal threads used, trellis stitch does not lend itself easily to experimentation by altering the scale of the grid. However, by using a variety of threads and clever use of colour, very interesting patterns can be built up. Smooth ribbons or metallic threads would look very effective. Light-coloured threads work well on a very dark background fabric. Alternatively, scraps of sheer or lurex fabrics could be applied to the background and then stitched over.

1. *First of all, lay down rows of straight horizontal stitches. Next, sew rows of vertical stitches in place. The spaces between the threads should all be equal if possible.*
2. *Diagonal threads are laid down, in one direction only.*
3. *A small diagonal stitch is used to tie down the layers of threads at each intersection.*

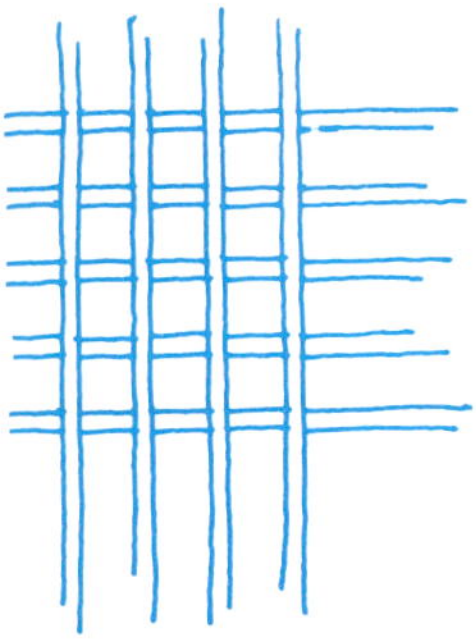

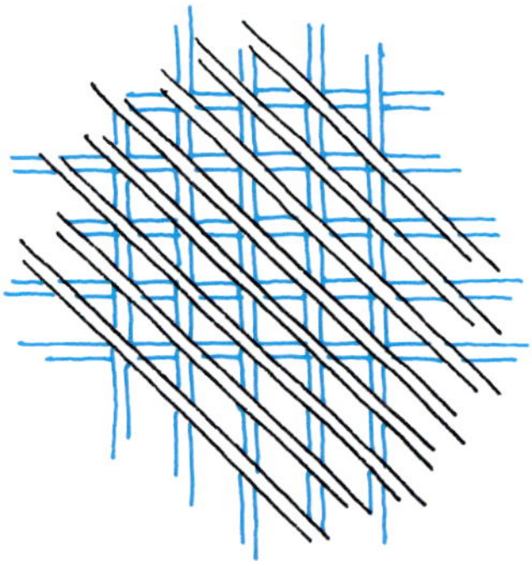

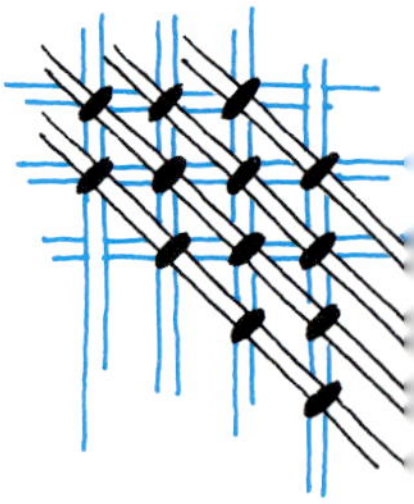

Cretan

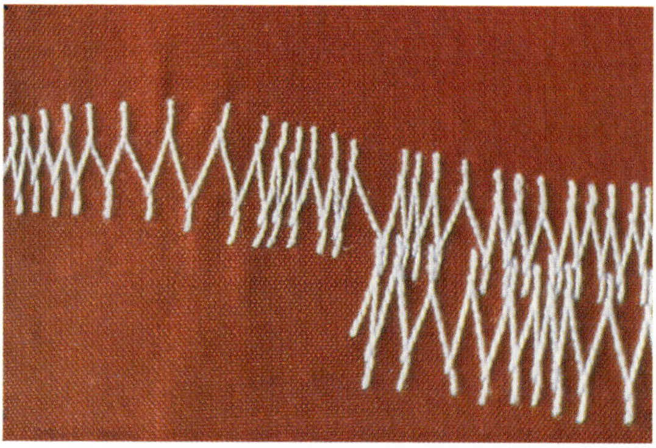

Cretan stitch is an immensely versatile stitch and very easy to work. It is essentially a border stitch but can be used to build up patterns and texture, such as foliage or masses of flowers. Any type of smooth thread can be used. Experiment with the stitches, working some close together and some far apart, and some very long stitches next to quite short ones. Work the stitches on top of each other in different threads and in varying thicknesses of threads. Tiny beads could be threaded into some of the stitches. For more experimental work, try cutting or tearing fabric into narrow strips and working Cretan stitch with these on a coarsely woven background fabric.

1. Bring the needle out through the fabric at A. Insert it at B and bring out again at C with the thread lying underneath the needle.
2. The stitch is then repeated at a point almost opposite and with the needle pointing upwards.

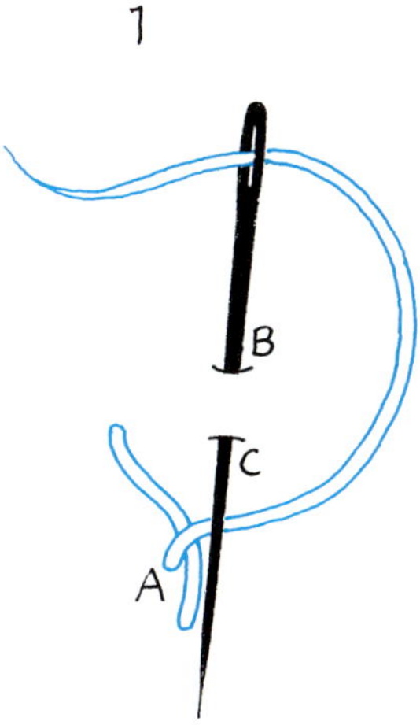

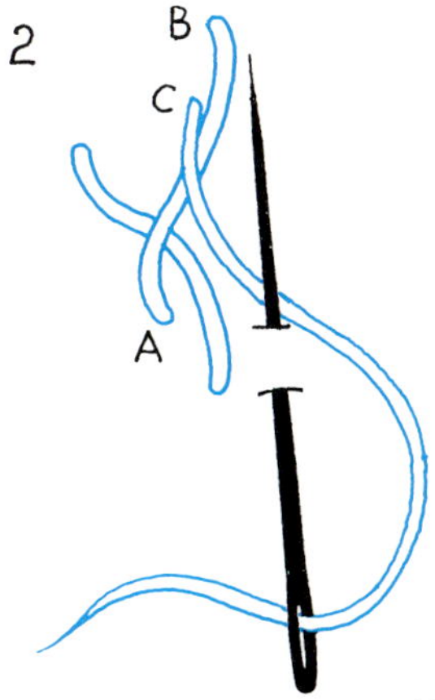

Cross

Cross stitch is generally thought of as a stitch used in counted thread embroidery. However, there is no reason why it cannot be used as a surface stitch on finer fabrics. If it is worked on a fabric without a noticeable warp and weft (e.g. calico, fine silk, etc) it will not, of course, be as neat and as accurate as when worked on a counted thread linen or linen substitute. 'Waste' canvas can be used if required. This is a canvas which is tacked over the fabric, the embroidery worked and then the canvas carefully removed. As well as being worked regularly and evenly, cross stitch forms interesting textures and patterns when worked freely. Experiment with an assortment of threads and work the stitches in a variety of sizes, making some of the stitches uneven, and build up layers by working stitches on top of each other.

1. Bring the needle out through the fabric at A. Insert the needle at B and bring out at C.
2. Insert the needle at D and bring out at E ready to work the next stitch.

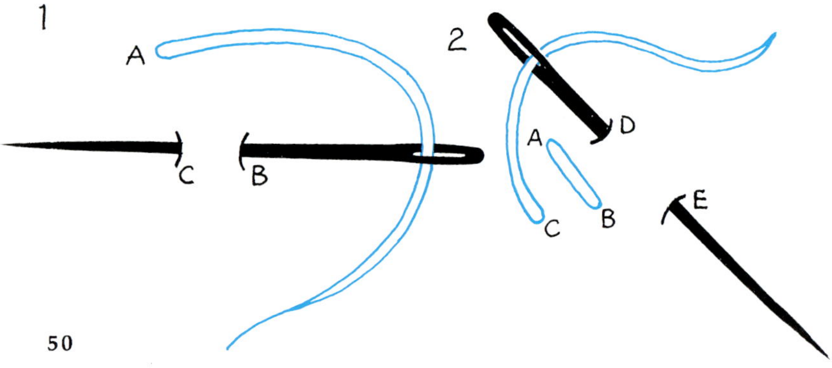

Darning

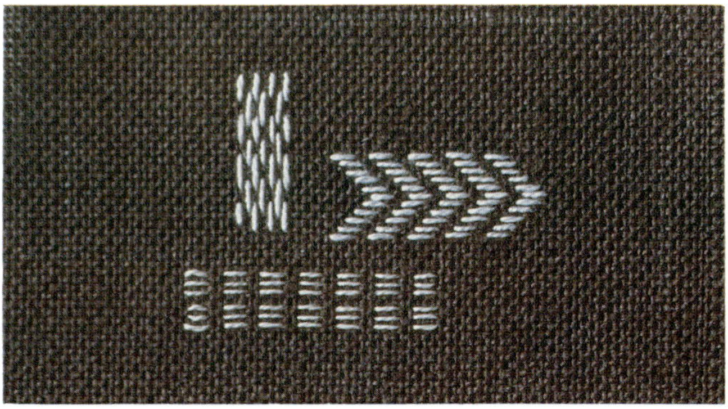

Darning is really pattern-making: rows of small, even running stitches are worked across the fabric to build up a variety of geometric patterns. When worked on non-evenweave fabrics it will, of course, be almost impossible to achieve absolute accuracy, but this adds to the charm. 'Waste' canvas can be used if such accuracy is required. This is canvas which is tacked over the fabric, the embroidery worked and then the canvas carefully removed. Before working darning patterns on fine fabric, practise making patterns on evenweave fabric. Try working on fine calico. Use smooth threads in a variety of colours; keep the stitches as regular and as even as possible. Darning patterns can also be worked on loosely woven fabrics such as curtain net, using thick threads, knitting yarns or even fabric torn into strips. It could also be tried on sheer organzas, when the stitches on the reverse side will also be visible.

Darning is a row of running stitches worked across the weave of the fabric. Keep the stitches and the spaces between the stitches as even as possible.

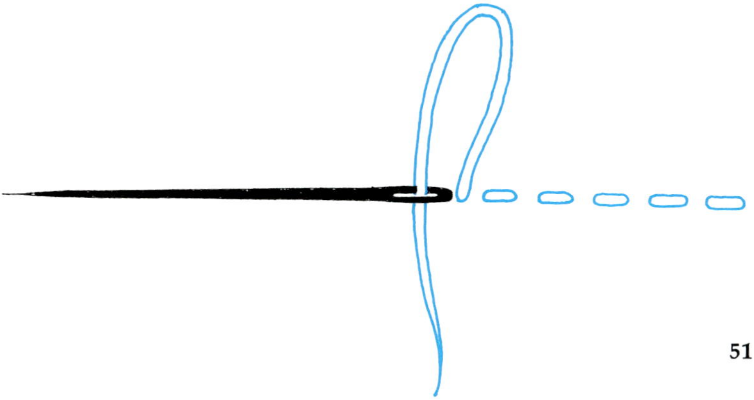

Dot

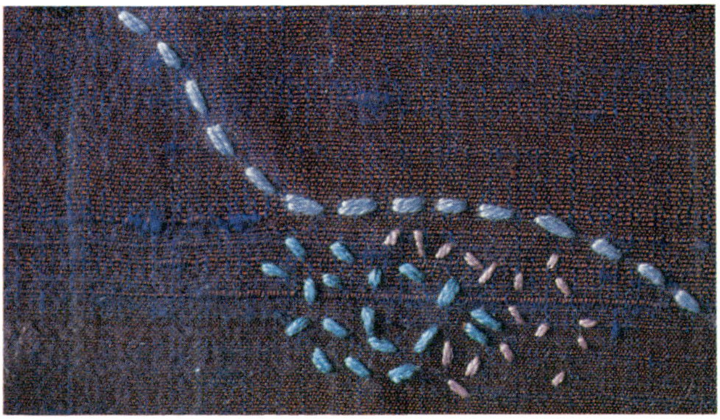

Dot stitch is a simple but very useful filling stitch. It is very similar to seeding or speckling and the stitches are often confused. It consists of two tiny back stitches worked in pairs. As well as a filling stitch, it can also be used as a line stitch, with a space left between the pairs of stitches, and it works especially well if a thickish thread is used. When used as a filling stitch it is best worked in a fine or medium-weight thread, or it can be overwhelming. Silk threads work particularly well. The stitches are worked in any direction, quite irregularly and of varying size.

Bring the needle out to the front of the fabric at A. Insert the needle at B and bring out again at A. Re-insert the needle at B to make a pair of stitches and bring it to the surface further along to begin working the next pair of stitches.

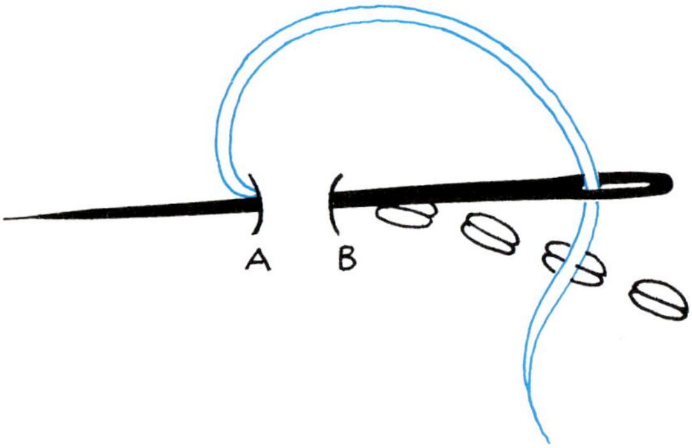

Double Knot

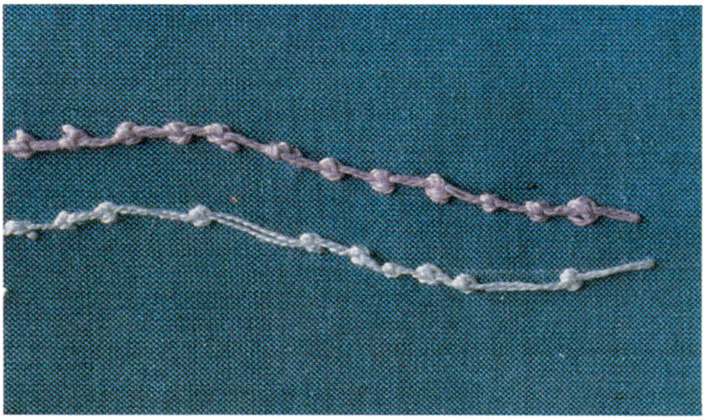

Similar in appearance to coral stitch, double knot stitch is rather more complicated to work and gives a more raised effect. It is often used as a border stitch, and is worked from left to right.

Experiment with threads and fabrics, although to begin with it is best to use a medium-weight fabric and medium-weight threads. Vary the thicknesses of the threads used and try working lines of the stitch so that they encroach on one another. Vary the spaces between the knots so that some knots are worked close together and others spaced apart. When several of the knots are massed together a very raised, textural stitch will be achieved.

1. Bring the needle out to the front of the fabric at A. Insert the needle at B and bring out again at C, forming a small horizontal stitch.

2. Pass the needle under this stitch, from the top. The needle should not pierce the fabric.

3. Pass the needle again through the stitch ensuring that the threads are placed under the needle. Again, the needle should not pierce the fabric.

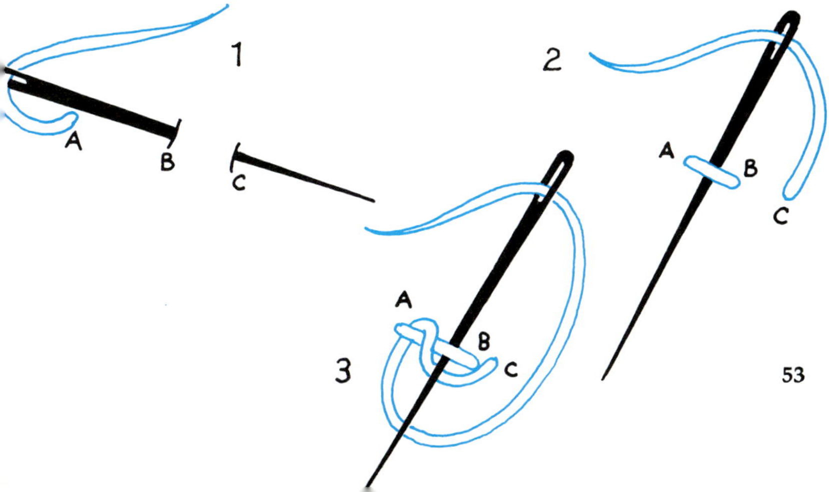

Ermine Filling

A simple stitch which builds up quickly, ermine filling consists of a long vertical stitch held in place with a cross stitch. It is used as a regular repeat pattern to cover large areas of ground fabric, usually in a half drop repeat pattern. It can be worked in most threads, although it is not very suitable for thick yarns. Try working the stitches in alternate colours. The spaces between the stitches can be varied, some stitches worked close together and some far apart, to give added interest.

1. *Bring the needle through to the surface of the fabric at A. Insert the needle at B and bring out again at C.*
2. *Re-insert the needle at D and bring out* again at E.
3. *Insert the needle at F and bring out again at G, ready to work the next stitch.*

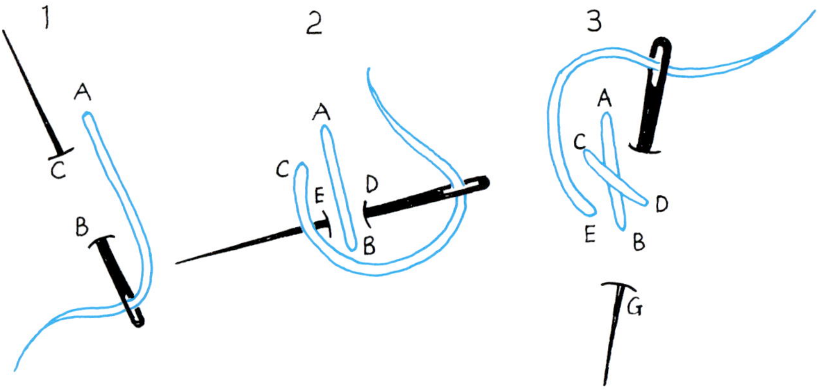

Eyelet

Although practice is needed to perfect it, this is an attractive filling stitch. The opportunities to experiment are limited but it is nevertheless quite useful in building up interesting shapes and patterns. Eyelet stitch is best worked in a fine or medium-weight thread. It works particularly well if a random dyed thread is used. To achieve a lacy effect, use a fine thread on larger circles. Use different-sized circles in a single design and place them so that the edges of the circles touch each other. On some circles the radial stitches could be quite close together and on others they could be spaced further apart.

To achieve accuracy, it is best first to trace a circle on to the fabric. Remember that each back stitch is worked twice into the same hole.

1. Bring out the needle to the front of the fabric at A, which is any point on the circumference. Insert the needle at B and bring out again at A. Repeat this stitch so that the needle is once again at A.

2. Insert the needle through the centre of the circle at C. Bring out again at A. Repeat, taking the needle through the centre but this time bring it out on the circumference a little further on from A, ready to work the next set of stitches.

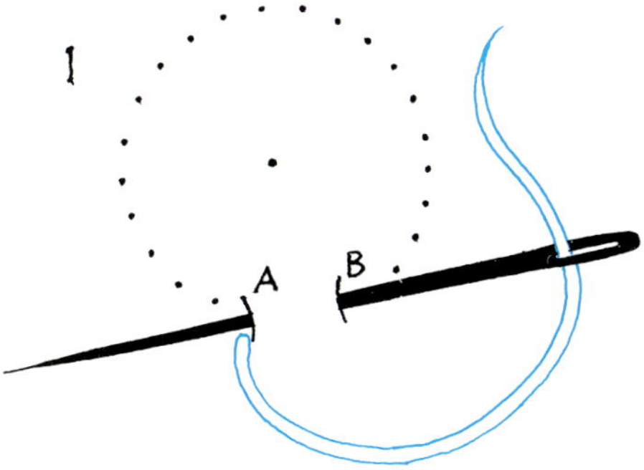

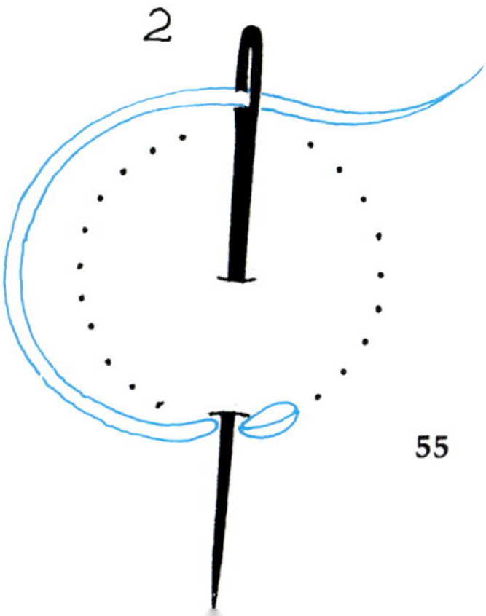

Eyelet stitch sampler worked by Vicky Lugg. The stitch has been worked in varying sizes using a combination of fine sewing cottons and metallic machine embroidery thread. Some of the stitches overlap each other. Shown here enlarged, the embroidered area is only 1.5 x 2 inches (3.5 x 5 cm).

The MADEIRA book of Needlepoint Miniatures presents as its subject Needlepoint in a new and attractive form. Fourteen miniature pictures to sew and frame are described in detail and illustrated in colour. There is a comprehensive stitch directory and a wealth of information for the inventive needlewoman.

The MADEIRA book of Needlepoint Stitches also by Susan Higginson, reflects the highly professional talents of this well known author. Containing 96 colour plates, this stitch directory provides detailed, step-by-step instructions in exploded view of all the stitches covered, making it a must for all involved in Canvas and Tapestry work.

Copies are available from MADEIRA stockists or direct from Madeira Threads (UK) Ltd.

MADEIRA

Cristal
MADEIRA
Embroidery Floss
Metallic
MADEIRA
No. 8
20 m
8010
Multi Star
Sequins-yarn
For Knitting and Decorative Use
MADEIRA

A whole new world of endless possibilities!

MADEIRA NO. 40

Madeira no. 40 is manufactured from 100% viscose with a very high tensile strength and an excellent silky lustre. Because of its unequaled finish, Madeira no. 40 is perfectly suited to use on high speed embroidery machines, profile stitchers, and all types of decorative stitchers. Madeira no. 40 is available in 240 beautiful lustrous colours and is supplied on 1100 yards (1000 m) spools or 5500 yards (5000 m) cones.
Article 911 - 1100 yds. (1000 m)/spool.
Article 910 - 5500 yds. (5000 m)/cone.

NEON NO. 40

Neon no. 40 is a 100% polyester embroidery thread with the same technical properties as our viscose rayon thread no. 40.
Neon no. 40 is for use on sports and safety wear, children's clothes, work clothes and for hotel linen. Is is available in 6 brilliant fluorescent and light reflective colours
Article 9845 - 220 yds. (200 m)/snap spool.

METALLIC THREAD NO. 40

Metallic thread no. 40 has a wide range of craft and decorative sewing uses. It is used for fine embroidery by hand or machine. Metallic no. 40 is available in 36 high fashion and opalescent colours.
Madeira has specially constructed this product enabling it to be used in the needle or as a bobbin thread.
Article 9842 - 220 yds. (200 m)/snap spool.

METALLIC SEWING THREAD NO. 15

Metallic sewing thread no. 15 is a strong, classical 3 ply metallic sewing thread used by industry on high speed sewing machines. It is supplied on 330 yards (20g) parallel wound spools in 3 shades of gold and silver.
Article 9815 - 330 yds. (20 g)/plastic reel.

METALLIC NO. 12

This metallic thread is intended for gold and silver work and for other hand embroidery uses. It can also be used for machine embroidery without difficulty. Available in silver and 2 shades of gold.
Article 9809 - 44 yds. (40 m)/snap spool.

METALLIC NO. 8

Metallic thread no. 8 is a braided effect thread for use in a wide range of crafts for ornamental, decoration and Christmas items. Metallic no. 8 is available in 3 shades of gold and 1 shade of silver and can be used in the bobbin of your sewing machine.
Article 9808 - 22 yds. (20 m)/snap spool.

METALLIC NO. 6

Metallic no. 6 is for use in gold work with broad application for couching and outlining. A pliable thread with numerous uses which can be used in the bobbin of your sewing machine. Available in 2 shades of gold and silver. This thread has wide uses in church embroidery, etc.
Article 9807 - 55 yds. (50 m)/snap spool.

METALLIC THREAD NO. 5

Metallic thread no. 5 is available in Madeira's special 22 yard (20 m) spiral pack in 5 antique colours of gold and silver. Metallic no. 5 is a thread that can be used in delicate embroidery or tapestry work or in the bobbin of your sewing machine.
It is also used for couching and for many other craft purposes.
Article 9805 - 22 yds. (20 m)/spiral pack.

METALLIC THREAD NO. 3

Metallic thread no. 3 is also supplied in Madeira's 22 yard (20 m) spiral pack. Ideally suited for couching, church embroidery, cord and braid making, book marks and the decorations of lampshades, making of tassels, etc., and in the bobbin of your sewing machine.
Metallic thread no. 3 is available in 4 bright colours of gold and silver.
Article 9803 - 22 yds. (20 m)/spiral pack.

TANNE NO. 50 - TEX 24

Tanne no. 50 is particularly suitable for fine and detailed embroidery on table linen, bed linen, hemming of hankerchiefs, on fine garments and for machine embroidery. Tanne no. 50 is available in 176 bright fashionable colours.
Article 950 - 5500 yds. (5000 m)/cone.
Article 951 - 1265 yds. (25 g)/cop.

TANNE NO. 30 - TEX 40

Tanne no. 30 is used by machine embroiderers to reduce the number of stitches in a design and for use on heavy fabrics. It is also used where a lower cost embroidery is required.
Tanne no. 30 is used for applique work, stitching on tackle twill letters, and for many decorative sewing operations where the lustre and quality of the thread is used to advantage.
Tanne no. 30 is available in 176 colours.
Article 930 - 5500 yds. (5000 m)/cone.
Article 931 - 714 yds. (25 g)/cop.

TANNE NO. 20 - TEX 60

Tanne no. 20 is mainly used to give a "hand embroidered" look to articles produced on embroidery machines. Tanne no. 20 is used for lacemaking, all counts, machine embroidery and crocheting.
It is also used to reduce stitch count on large embroidery design.
Tanne no. 20 is available in 66 colours.
Article 920 - 5500 yds. (5000 m)/cone.
Article 921 - 495 yds. (25 g)/cop.

TANNE NO. 12 - TEX 76

Tanne no. 12 is used for serging and smocking, picot edging on a variety of garments and is used on various embroidery machines. Tanne no. 12 is available in 60 beautiful colours.
Article 960 - 2750 yds. (2500 m)/cone.
Article 961 - 385 yds. (25 g)/cop.

DECOR NO. 6

Decor no. 6 is Madeira's high fashion 100% viscose knitting accompanying yarn which can be used with 1, 2 or more ends to give that "something extra" to the design of a knitted garment. The high lustre and soft look of Decor provides a whole new world of exciting possibilities and is the #1 thread used in the upper looper of your serger.
Decor no. 6 is available in 36 eye catching colours.
Article 9806 - 207 yds. (25 g)/ spool.

MADEIRA 6 STRAND COTTON.

Produced from Egyptian long staple cotton, this high quality MADEIRA 6 strand embroidery cotton is double mercerised and fast-dyed to 95 deg. C to give that soft handle and silky lustre to enhance your needlework. MADEIRA's packaging is modern in concept, the thread is kept clean and tangle-free at all times and contains 10 metres of thread, which is 25% more quality thread than the standard 8 metre traditional skein. There are 324 beautiful colours in the MADEIRA 6 strand cotton range.

4 STRAND PURE SILK.

MADEIRA 4 strand pure silk embroidery floss, your precious needlework deserves the best. See your dreams come true with 104 brilliant colours. Ideal for all needleworks. Supplied in MADEIRA's tangle-free spiral packaging containing 5 metres of this excellent product.

MADEIRA

RAYON NO. 40.

Rayon No. 40, the premier high quality machine embroidery thread from MADEIRA. This product is used by the majority of Industrial machine embroiderers and has been in use for many years. A lustrous thread, produced from high tensile strength rayon on 200 metre snap spools and available in 60 colours.

MADEIRA

Feather

A simple stitch which is very versatile, and traditionally used as a border stitch on children's garments. Although a linear stitch, it can be used as an all-over pattern and is especially useful when working gardens or landscapes. Any type of thread can be used, from fine sewing cotton to thick yarns (although, of course, these can only be used on fabrics with a loose weave). The stitches can be worked quite regularly and evenly, or interesting effects can be achieved by combining very large stitches with very small ones. Work lines of stitches on top of each other, using a variety of threads, to build up textures and patterns.

The stitch is worked in a vertical line, from top to bottom. Bring the needle out of the fabric at A. Insert the needle at B, which is to the right of A, and bring out again at C, with the working thread lying under the needle. The next stitch is formed in the same way, but the needle should be inserted to the left of C, at a distance equal to AB.

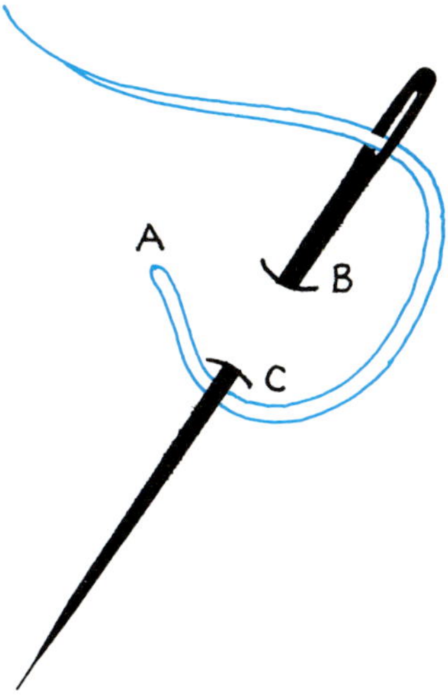

Double Feather

Worked in the same way as feather stitch, but forming a much broader line. Instead of making a single stitch to the right and then to the left, two, three, or more stitches are made before changing direction. Thus quite large areas of fabric can be covered very quickly. Experiment with a variety of threads from fine cottons to thick knitting yarns, although these should only be used on fabrics with a loose weave. The stitches can be worked quite regularly and evenly, or more interesting effects can be achieved by combining very large stitches with very small ones. Work rows of stitches on top of each other using a variety of threads, to build up textures and patterns. Vary the stitches worked so that several are worked one way and perhaps only one in the opposite direction.

As in feather stitch, work from top to bottom. Bring the needle out through the fabric at A. Insert the needle at B and bring out again at C, with the working thread lying under the needle. The next stitch will be worked in the same way, with the needle inserted to the right of C. After two or three stitches have been worked in this way, the needle can then be inserted in the fabric to the left of the stitch so that the line changes direction.

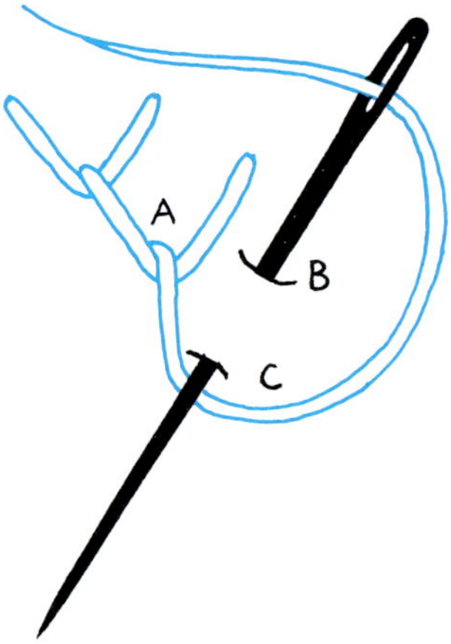

Fern

Fern stitch is a very simple, attractive stitch, and, as its name suggests, is extremely useful when working flowers or foliage.

It is really no more than three straight stitches with the bases of the stitches meeting at the same point. The stitch can be worked in a variety of threads, from very fine cottons to thick knitting yarns. Vary the size of the stitch so that some stitches are very small and in other areas are spaced further apart, to produce a lacy effect. To produce a foliage effect, work lines of stitchery in very fine threads on top of one another.

1. *Bring the needle out to the front of the fabric at A. Insert at B and bring out again at C.*

2. *Insert the needle at D (same point as A) and bring out again at E. Re-insert the needle at D to complete the stitch.*

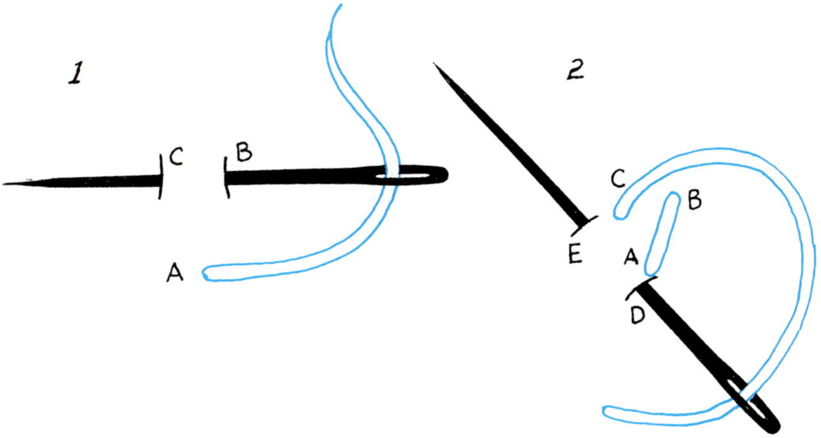

Fishbone

Although this is traditionally a filling stitch it can also be used as a border, although it is a little difficult to achieve an evenly sized stitch. As the stitches are usually worked very close together, it is not particularly suitable for thicker threads. Try a medium-weight thread – possibly silk or a random dyed thread. Fishbone stitch is also often used as a leaf-filling stitch, and can be very successful when a heavily textured area is required. Experiment with this by working the stitch quite freely, and working stitches on top of each other. Fishbone stitch is usually worked from top to bottom.

1. Bring the needle out to the front of the fabric at A. Insert it at B and bring out again at C.

2. Re-insert the needle at D so that it crosses the first stitch. Bring the needle out again just below A, ready to work the next stitch.

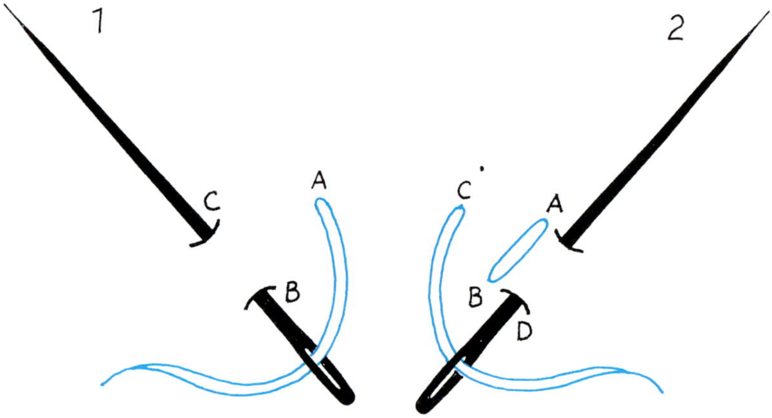

Fly

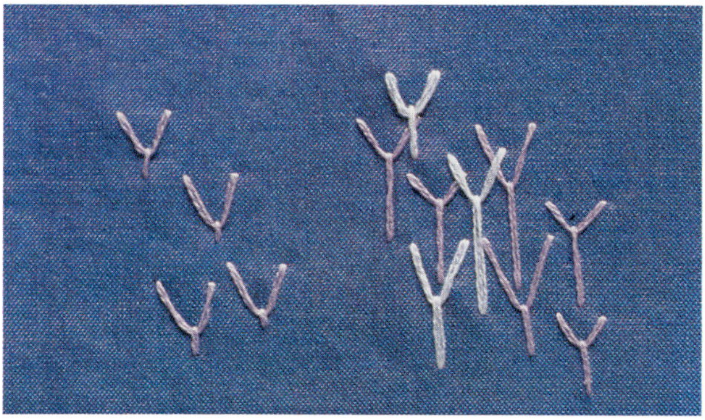

Fly stitch is a simply worked stitch, which can be used to build up textures or as a regular all-over pattern. Any smooth thread can be used, from fine machine threads to thick knitting yarns and even torn fabric strips. The 'tail' of the stitch can be left quite long, as shown above, to provide added interest.

Use an assortment of different thicknesses of threads to build up textured areas, starting with thick threads and finishing with very fine silks or machine threads.

1. Bring the needle out to the front of the fabric at A. Insert it at B and bring out again at C with the working thread lying under the needle.

2. Insert the needle at D and bring out again at E ready to commence the next stitch.

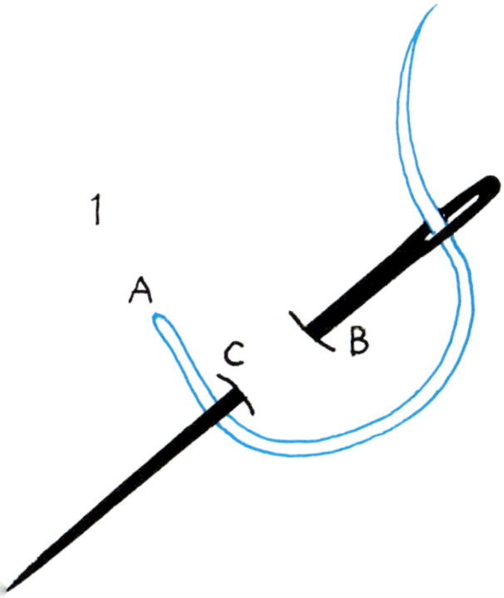

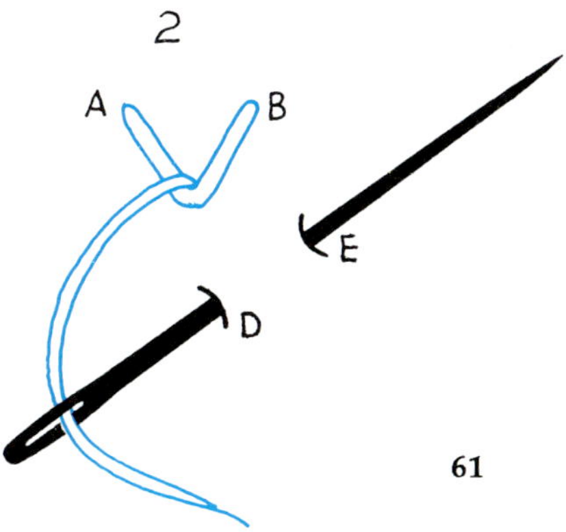

Four Legged Knot

This is a simple stitch to work, useful in building up textures or as a regular all-over pattern. Four legged knot is actually a combination of an upright cross stitch and a coral knot. Smooth threads should be used but these can be of any thickness, from fine sewing cottons to thicker knitting yarns. It is traditionally worked as a regular repeat pattern but it can be massed together to build up textured areas, and is useful when depicting flowers or foliage. Use a variety of thicknesses of threads and combine shiny threads with matt threads.

1. Bring the needle out to the surface at A and insert at B. Bring the needle out again at C.

2. Take the needle under the centre of the straight stitch without piercing the fabric. The working thread should be looped under the needle. To complete the stitch, take the needle through the fabric at D.

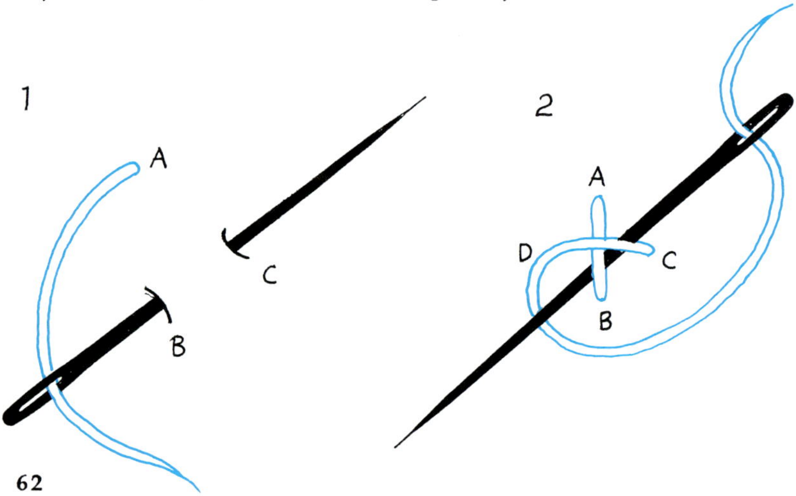

French Knot

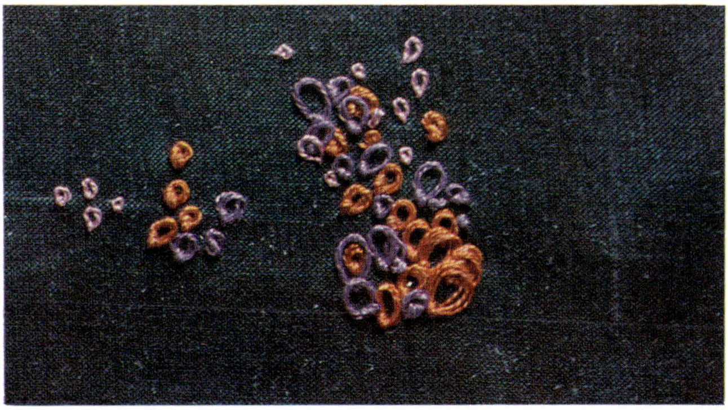

French knot is an extremely useful stitch, widely found as a textured filling stitch and in embroideries of gardens or landscapes. Although practice is needed to work it correctly, it is not nearly as difficult as bullion knot. When first working this stitch it is advisable to use a thread that is not too tightly twisted, as this will make the stitch difficult to work. French knots can be worked in a wide variety of threads, although textured threads are not very suitable. It looks particularly effective when worked in different weight threads and massed together to produce interesting textures. To obtain other interesting effects contrast matt threads with shiny silks or rayon threads. Work some of the stitches so that loops are left on the surface.

French knots can also be used as a simple border decoration, possibly as part of another stitch, such as guilloche stitch.

Bring the needle through to the surface of the fabric at A. Twist the thread once around the needle as shown in the diagram, and re-insert the needle into the fabric at A, making sure that the thread stays twisted around the needle.

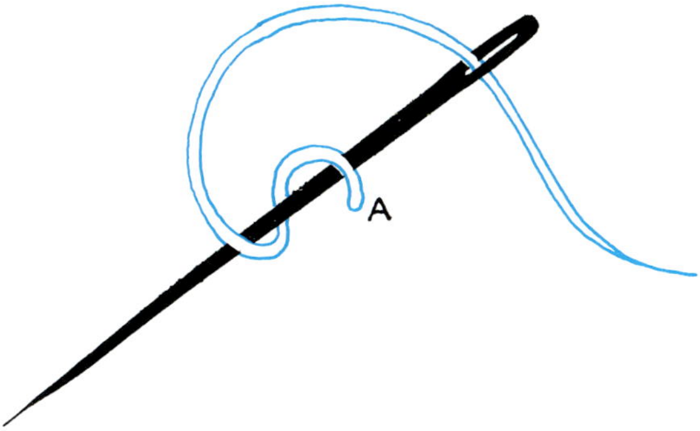

Guilloche

Guilloche stitch is actually several stitches combined to make an attractive border pattern. The stitches used are very simple ones, and the composite is not difficult to work, although care should be taken to ensure that it is fairly even. It is quite a formal stitch and its uses are restricted. Choose medium-weight threads, although varying the thicknesses of the threads gives a more interesting effect. Choose the colours carefully: tones of the same colour are effective, or you could work part of the stitch (perhaps the French knots) in a contrasting thread.

First work the two outer rows of stem stitch. Next, work a row of small straight stitches, formed of evenly spaced groups of three horizontal stitches worked underneath each other. A thread is then looped between these groups of stitches, first in one direction and then back again to fill in the spaces. The needle should not pierce the fabric. Finally a French knot is worked in the space between each loop.

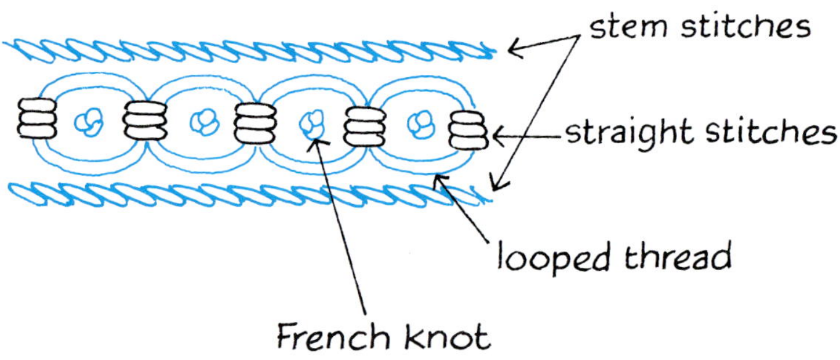

Herringbone

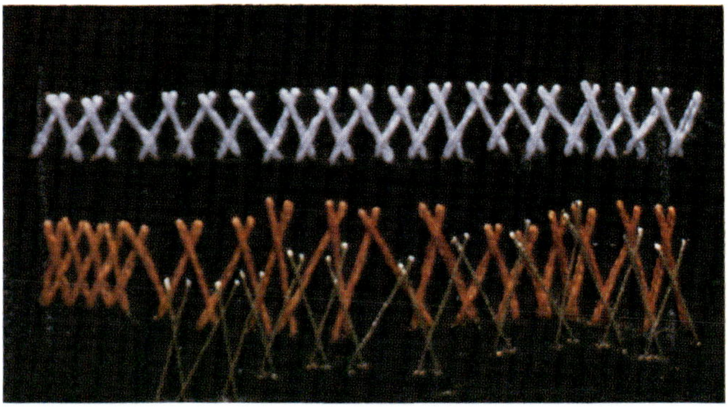

Herringbone is a useful linear stitch, simple to work and ideal for experimentation. As well as a surface stitch, it is the traditional stitch used in shadow work, when it is worked on the reverse of the fabric so that two parallel rows of small back stitches appear on the surface and the vertical stitches appear as shadowy lines.

Any kind of thread can be used, from very fine to quite thick threads, although textured yarns are not particularly suitable. Experiment by working some of the stitches close together and others further apart. Vary the length of the stitches so that some are very long. Work rows of herringbone stitch on top of each other in contrasting colours and varying thicknesses of threads. The stitch is worked from left to right.

1. Bring the needle out at A. Insert the needle at B and bring out again at C.

2. Re-insert the needle at D and bring out again at E ready to work the next stitch.

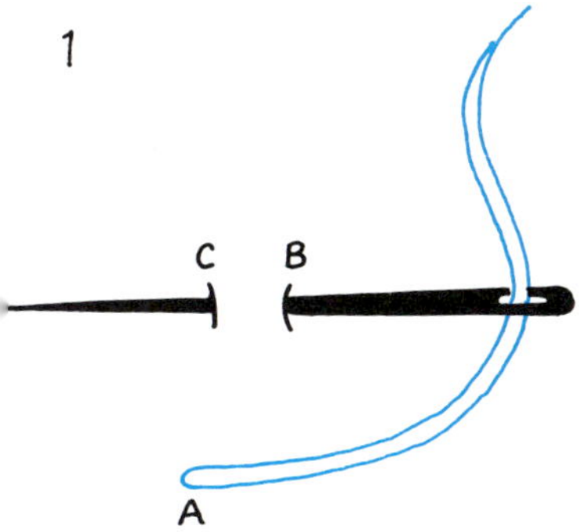

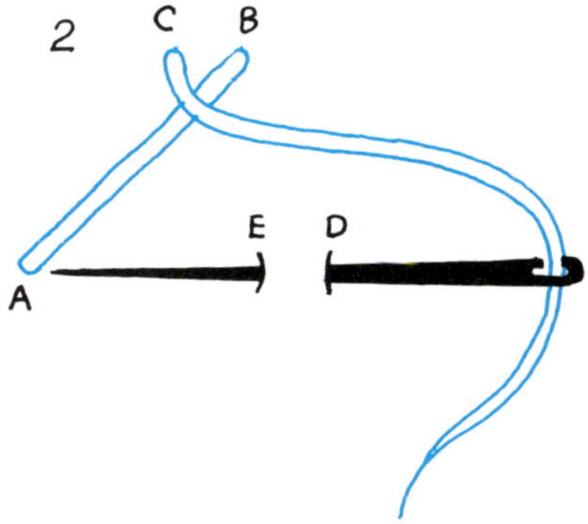

Threaded Herringbone

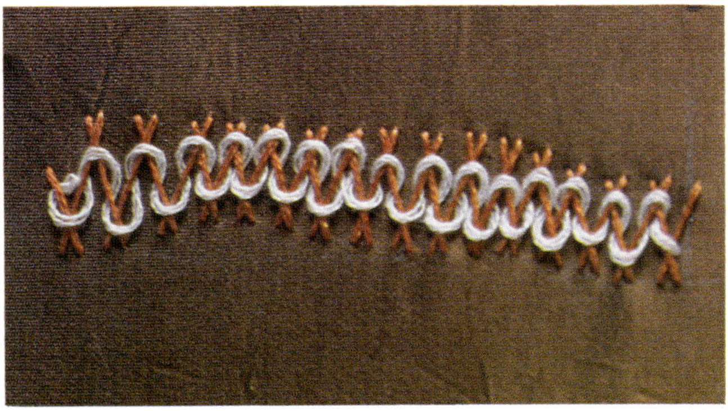

This is one of several versions of herringbone stitch, often used as a border pattern worked in two contrasting colours. Any kind of thread can be used, from very fine to quite thick threads. Textured yarns could be used to thread over the foundation stitches, as they do not pierce the fabric. As with herringbone stitch, experiment by working some of the stitches close together and others spaced apart. Vary the length of the stitches and overlap the rows as they are worked. As the threaded stitch is worked, the base threads may be pulled quite tightly to distort them further.

Work a row of herringbone stitches as a foundation. Lace a second thread, usually a contrasting colour, through the foundation stitches, as shown in the diagram. The needle should not pierce the fabric.

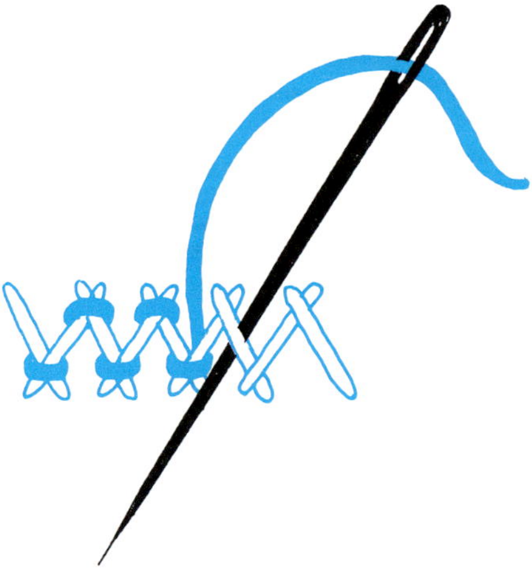

Holbein

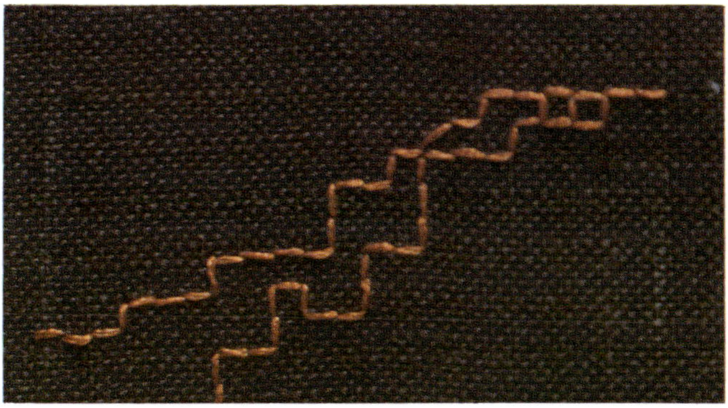

Often known as double running stitch, Holbein stitch is the principal stitch used in blackwork embroidery. It is usually worked on an evenweave fabric, and although it can be worked on a finely woven fabric, care should be taken to ensure that the stitches are as even and as regular as possible. It is best to work with a fairly fine or medium-weight thread. Traditionally, a black thread is used but experiment with other colours. Try building up irregular geometric patterns, using more than one colour thread or tones of the same colour. Holbein stitch is very useful when working buildings.

Holbein stitch is worked in two parts. A row of running stitches is worked in one direction; the space between the stitches should be the same size as the actual stitches. A return row is then worked, stitching over the spaces made by the first row so that the stitch shows as a continuous solid line.

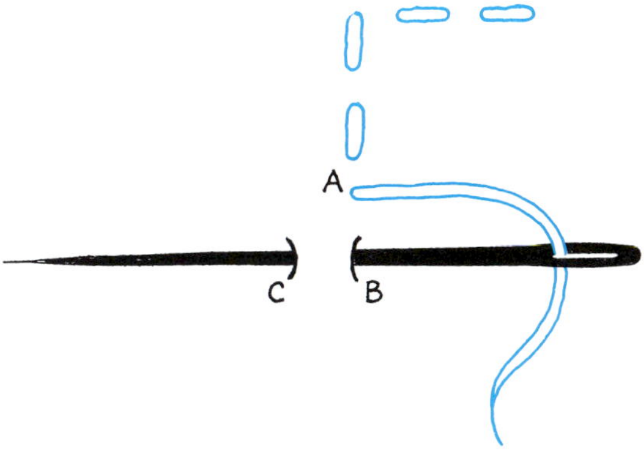

Japanese Darning

This can also be used as a quilting stitch. The stitches should be quite large so it is relatively quickly worked. Its origins are found on traditional Japanese peasant garments, where the stitching was usually worked in white thread on an indigo dyed fabric. Two or more layers of fabric were often stitched together with rows of simple geometric patterns to provide extra warmth as well as surface decoration. Of course, it is not necessary to work the stitchery in white thread, but it does look very attractive if a colour contrasting with the background fabric is used. It is possible to build up quite elaborate all-over patterns.

1. Work two or more rows of running stitches. The stitches in the second row should overlap those of the first row, the spaces between the stitches being usually smaller than the stitches.

2. A third row of stitches is then worked, to join the first two rows together.

1

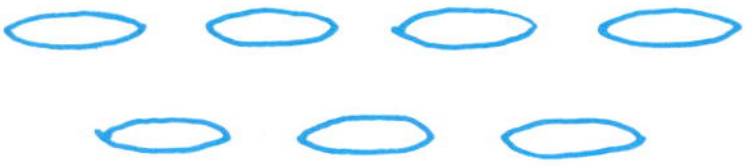

2

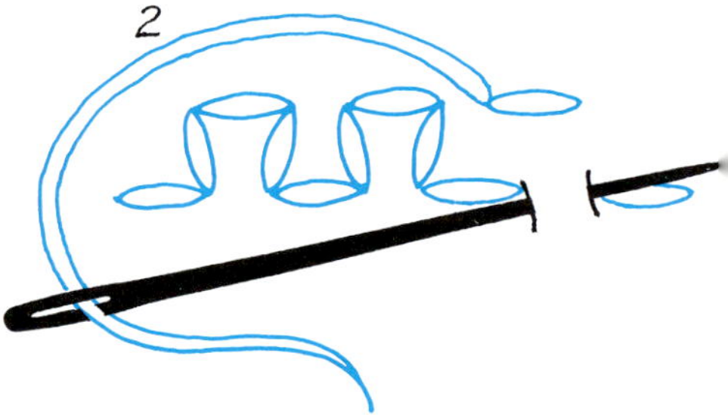

Laid Work

This is a traditional pattern, often used for flowers or leaves in crewel embroidery. Fine crewel wools or floss silks were used. However, floss silk is now almost unobtainable and is also extremely difficult to handle. Any smooth embroidery thread is suitable, although it should be quite fine. A trellis work of geometric patterns is built up over a foundation of long stitches which entirely cover the shape. The patterns are usually regular but need not be so. Instead of tying the threads down with cross stitches or small back stitches, try French knots at each intersection, or beads or sequins.

1. First, a foundation of long straight stitches is worked to cover the entire shape.

2. With a contrast thread geometric patterns are then laid over the top, usually at an angle to the first row. These threads are in turn secured at each intersection with a tiny decorative stitch, often cross stitch.

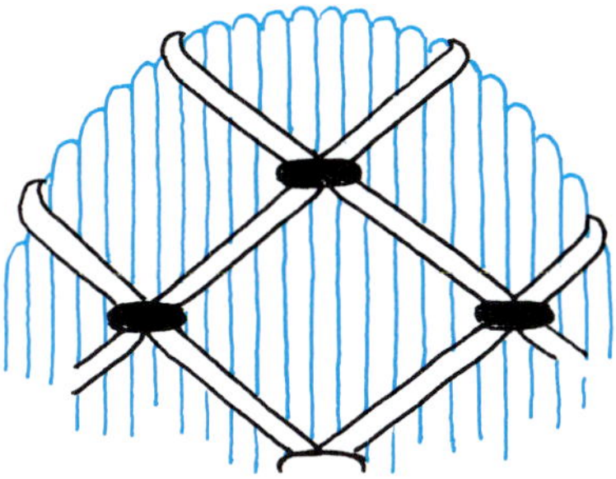

Leaf

As suggested by its name, this stitch is often used as a filling for leaf shapes. It is similar to fishbone stitch but the stitches should not be worked so closely together. It can be very successful when building up textured areas, especially when working gardens or flowers. Experiment with a variety of thicknesses of threads. Build up heavily textured areas by working the stitch quite freely, and working stitches on top of each other. Leaf stitch is worked from the bottom to the top.

1. Bring the needle out to the front of the fabric at A. Insert it at B and bring out again at C.

2. Insert the needle at D and bring out again at E, which is above and slightly to the left of A.

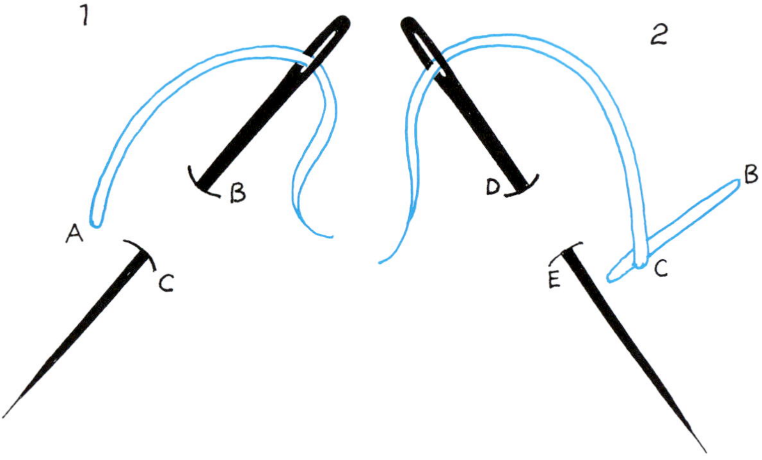

Lock

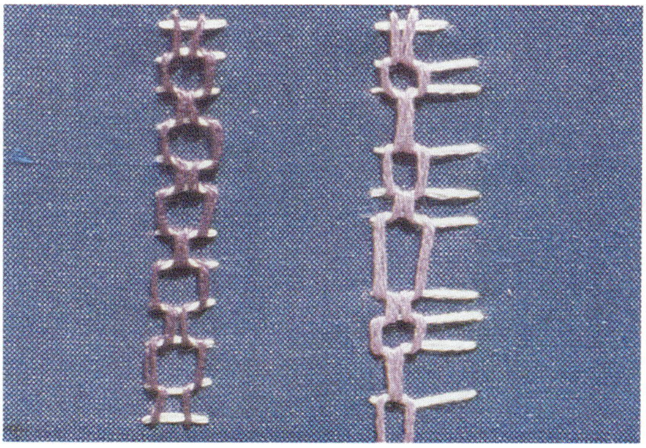

Lock stitch is a little-used stitch which is, however, quite simple to work and very versatile. Like other composite stitches, it is worked on a base of horizontal stitches. Smooth, medium-weight threads are best to use for this part of the stitch but thicker threads can be used. Textured threads can be used for the second stage as the thread does not pass through the background fabric. Traditionally, the ladder stitches are spaced at regular intervals, but working some close together and others much further apart will result in an attractive irregular stitch. Beads can be incorporated to give added textural interest.

1. The first stage is a row of horizontal straight stitches.

2. The needle does not pierce the fabric for this part of the stitch. Starting at the top, take the thread over the first two stitches and out at A. Keeping the thread to the right, bring the needle out at B. Repeat for the next stitch, but keep the thread to the left of the needle. When the first row has been worked, return to the top of the work and repeat, but so that two stitches come close together, then two far apart, as shown in the photograph.

1

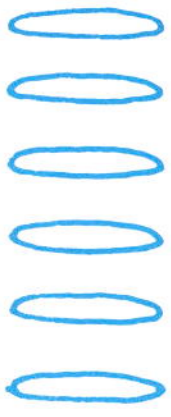

2

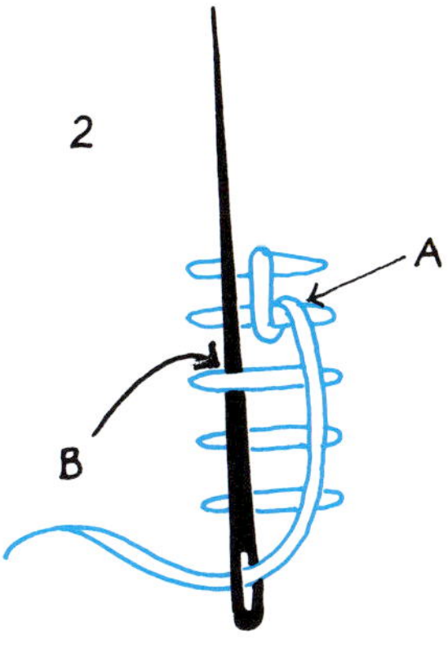

Long and Short

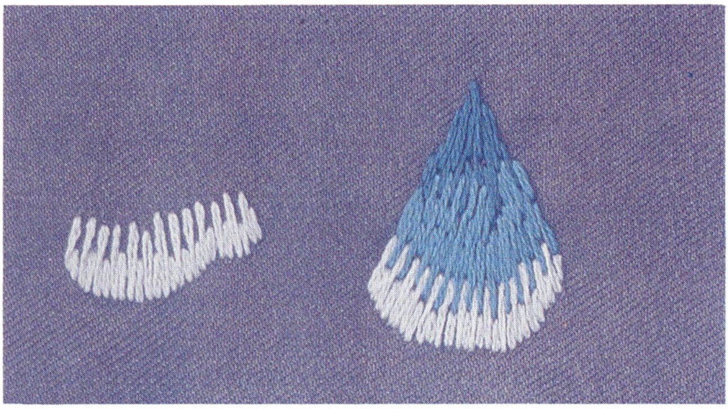

Long and short is a traditional embroidery stitch often used as shading when working flowers and plants. Floss silk was traditionally used to work this stitch, but it is now virtually impossible to obtain and very difficult to use. Any fine embroidery threads are suitable, especially stranded silks, which will give the embroidery the required sheen. Long and short stitch is very useful when working areas of embroidery that need careful shading. It is not very difficult to work but requires care to obtain an even, regular stitch.

The area to be worked should first be outlined: the easiest way to do this is to work a row of tiny running stitches around the edge.

1. *On the first row, a long and a short stitch should be worked alternately.*
2. *On the next and subsequent rows, only long stitches are worked and these should fit neatly into the spaces made on the previous row, so that the stitches all merge together.*

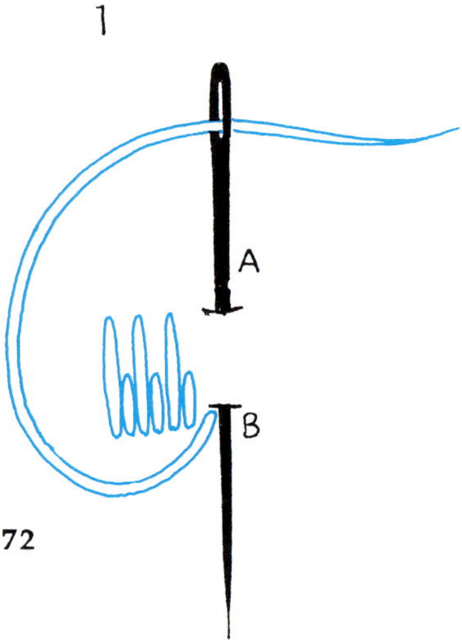

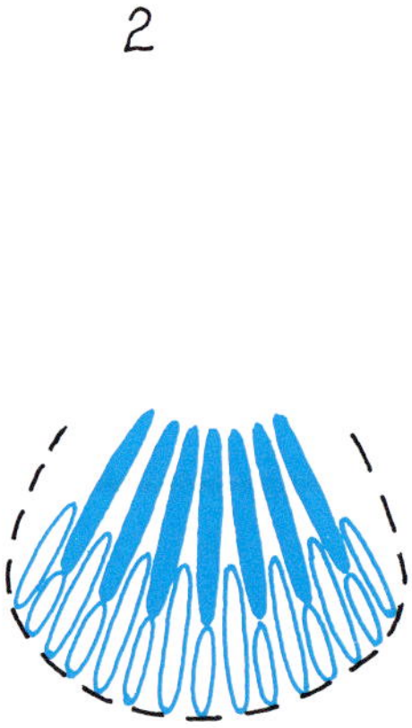

Free Machining

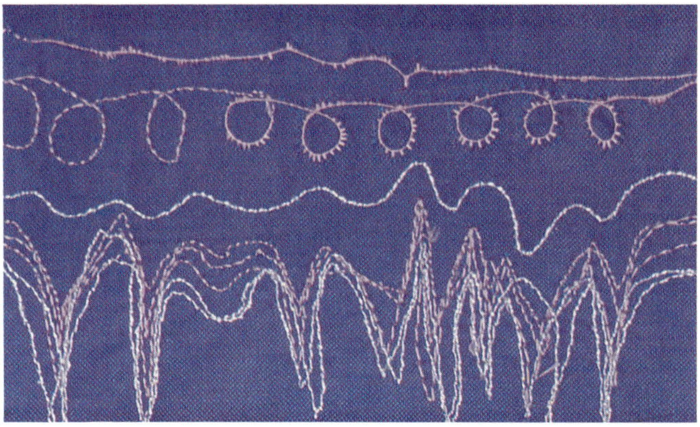

This is the first of three free machine techniques described in this book. Any straight-stitch domestic sewing machine can be used for these stitches, but as instructions vary, it is recommended that the machine instruction book is referred to. A plentiful supply of machine needles and machine embroidery threads will also be needed.

The presser foot should first be removed. Some machines are provided with a darning foot which is excellent for free embroidery. Next, lower or cover the feed dog (some sewing machines have a plate for this purpose). Set the stitch length to 0 and use a size 90 or 100 needle.

Place the fabric in a ring frame so that it is absolutely drum tight and sits flat on the bed of the sewing machine.

Manually turn the fly wheel so that the needle is inserted into the fabric and the bobbin thread is brought up to the surface.

Lower the presser foot lever. It is very important to do this and it is easier to remember if a darning foot is used rather than no foot at all.

Begin stitching, moving the framed fabric carefully to obtain patterns and designs. At first do not move the frame too fast, but with practice it will be possible to build up considerable speed.

Cable

Cable stitch is used when sewing thick threads that cannot be used on the top of the sewing machine. These threads are wound by hand on to the bobbin and the fabric will be placed face down during the sewing process. As it involves loosening the lower tension, cable stitch should be used with care, as it is sometimes difficult to return the tension to its normal setting. Some sewing machines have a separate bobbin case, and it is worth investing in a second case, removing the screw that provides the tensioning and keeping the case solely for free machining.

To work cable stitch, the top tension should be set at 'normal'. Remove the presser foot and lower or cover the feed dog (some sewing machines have a plate for this purpose). Set the stitch length to 0 and use a size 90 or 100 needle. Loosen the lower tension (refer to the machine guide book) but take great care to remember where the normal tension setting should be. When using thick hand-embroidery threads it will be necessary to wind the bobbin by hand.

Place the fabric in a ring frame with the right side of the fabric facing down on the sewing machine. Ensure that the fabric is drum tight in the frame.

Manually turn the fly wheel so that the needle is inserted into the fabric and the bobbin thread is brought up to the surface. Lower the presser foot lever.

Begin stitching, moving the frame carefully and steadily.

LEFT **York** *This sampler was based on a photograph of a paving slab found in an old church in York. The embroidery is a combination of hand and machine stitching on layers of sheer fabric applied to a background of unbleached calico. The free machining has been worked in metallic and rayon embroidery threads and the hand stitching in silk threads using running, cross and seeding stitch. Embroidered area: 4 x 7.25 inches (10 x 18 cm).*

Whip

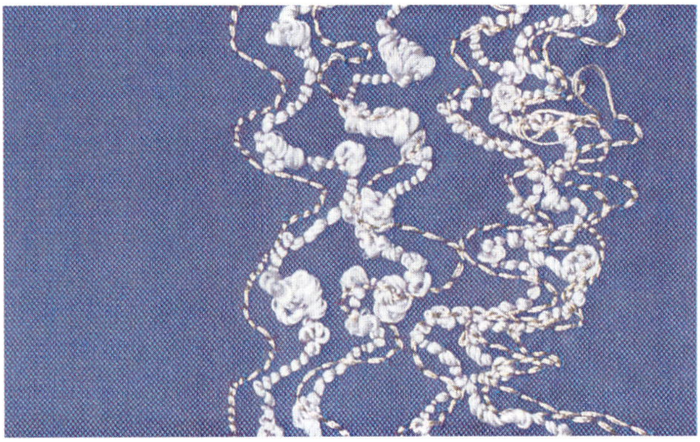

This is the next stage in free machining. Whip stitch will produce a more textured stitch than the previous two, and as in cable stitch, the bobbin thread will appear on the surface of the fabric. It is worth experimenting by winding a variety of threads on to the bobbin to see the different effects you can achieve.

To work whip stitch, the top tension must be tightened (refer to the machine guide for instructions). As described on the previous page, the presser foot should be removed. Lower or cover the feed dog (some sewing machines have a plate for this purpose). Set the stitch length to 0 and use a size 90 or 100 needle.

Place the fabric in a ring frame so that it is absolutely drum tight and sits flat on the bed of the sewing machine.

Manually turn the fly wheel so that the needle is inserted into the fabric and the bobbin thread is brought up to the surface. Lower the presser foot lever.

Begin stitching, gradually tightening the top tension until the bobbin thread appears on the surface as a ridged line. If the top thread continually snaps, loosen the tension slightly. The best results will be obtained by running the machine quite fast and moving the frame quite slowly.

Landscape worked by Diane Capp. The fields and sky have been drawn with coloured pencils. The trees and hedgerows are worked in machine embroidery and the flowers, stems and sheep have been added in hand stitchery, using very fine threads. Embroidered area: 2.75 x 4.5 inches (7 x 11 cm).

Outline

This stitch is simple and quick to work and can be used for depicting curved lines in flowers or foliage or any figurative work. It is very similar to stem stitch, except that the thread is always kept to the left of the needle. Any smooth thread can be used, including knitting and weaving yarns if the weave of the background fabric is loose enough. Experiment by working the stitch in different lengths: some very small stitches with some very long stitches. Work lines of outline stitch close together and on top of each other so that textured effects can be achieved. Combine shiny threads with dull, matt threads.

It is important to remember to keep the working thread always to the left of the needle. The stitch is worked from bottom to top.

Bring the needle out to the surface of the fabric at A. Insert at B and bring out again at C, so that the stitches slightly overlap each other.

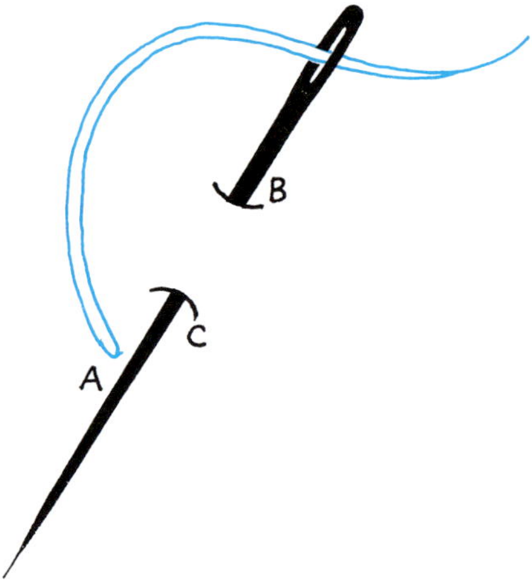

Overcast

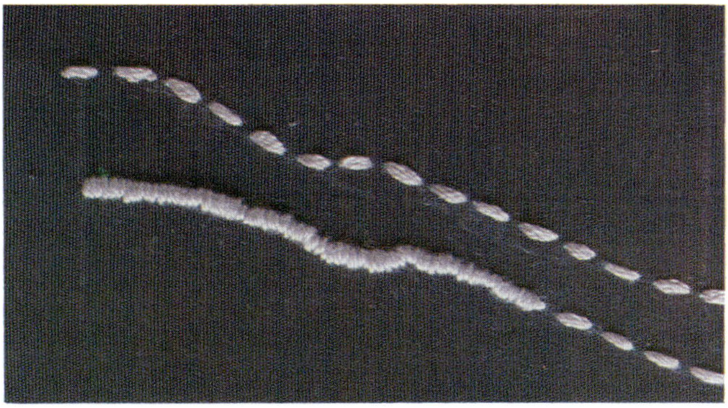

This is a very useful stitch, but some care is needed to achieve a good effect. It was traditionally used when embroidering monograms, as it gives a firm raised line. A fairly fine smooth thread should be used (it is extremely difficult to work in stranded cottons); a random dyed thread can be very attractive, and a more raised effect can be achieved if the running stitches are worked in a thick thread.

It looks well if used in conjunction with smooth stitches, and rows of stitches worked close together in contrasting or toning threads make interesting patterns.

1. A row of running stitches must first be worked, with very little space between the stitches.

2. A row of tiny stitches is then worked over the running stitches. The needle is inserted into the background fabric with each stitch, and the stitches should be placed close together so that the core thread does not show.

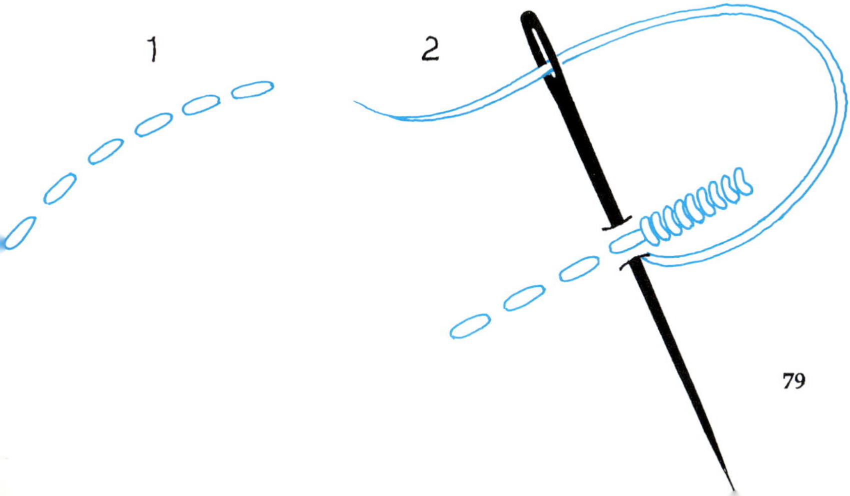

Pekinese

A line stitch which is quick and easy to work and produces quite a wide, attractive border. A smooth thread should be used for the back stitches, but as the interlaced thread does not pierce the fabric, any interesting textured thread can be used for this, including weaving yarns. It is particularly effective if a metallic thread is used. Traditionally the loops of the interlacing thread should be pulled quite tightly, but the stitch becomes much more interesting if quite large loops are left on the surface of the fabric.

1. *A row of back stitches must first be worked.*

2. *Then the interlaced thread is worked from left to right, passing beneath the second stitch, back beneath the first stitch, then forward, to pass beneath the third stitch, and so on, as shown in the diagram. The needle should not pierce the fabric.*

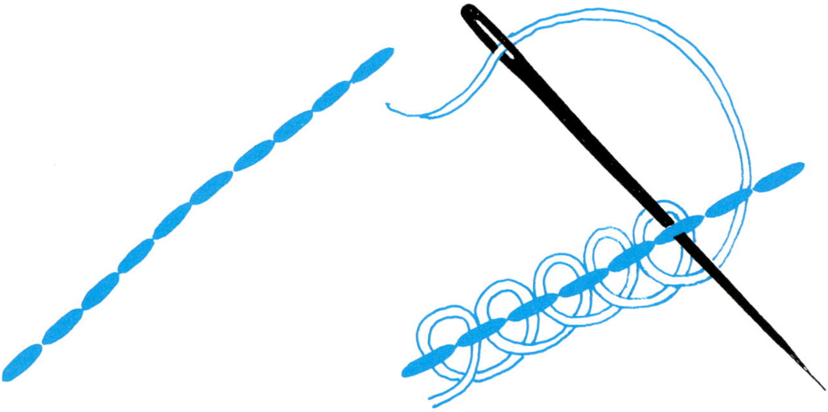

Petal

This very attractive stitch is composed of detached chain and stem stitch. Although at first glance it looks very complicated, it is in fact very simple to work. Petal stitch is little used, but can be very effective when used for flowers or foliage, for curving lines and for building up patterns. A smooth medium-weight thread is best, and it looks well in shiny silks or random dyed threads. Experiment with the detached chain stitches, working them very close together or spaced further apart. Work some very tiny chain stitches next to very long stitches. Try building rows of stitches on top of each other to see what textural effects can be achieved.

1. Bring the needle out to the surface of the fabric at A. Insert it at B and bring out again at C.

2. Re-insert the needle at C, and bring out at D with the working thread looped beneath the needle.

3. Insert the needle at E and bring out again at F near A, ready to work the next stitch.

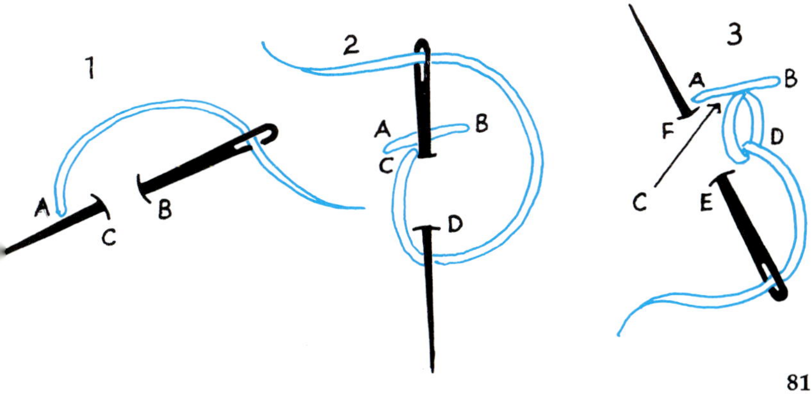

Portuguese Border

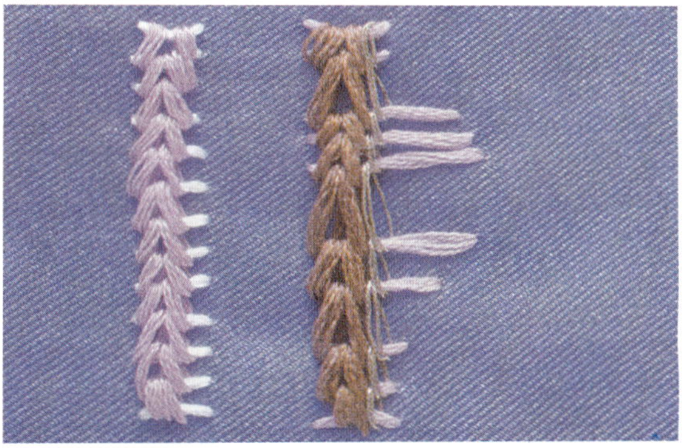

This forms quite a wide border. It is not difficult to work but care needs to be taken with the tension. Firm, medium-weight threads are best, but thicker yarns can be used and interesting textures achieved. Contrasting or toning threads and shiny and matt threads of the same colour can all be used. The foundation stitches can be spaced unequally, and if they are very wide you can work several rows of stitchery into the same band, using a variety of threads. Metallic threads work well.

1. A vertical row of straight stitches must first be worked. Working from bottom to top work four satin stitches over the first two bars (see photograph above).

2. Bring the needle out to the top left of these satin stitches at A. Without piercing the fabric, insert the needle down through the next two bars, keeping the working thread to the right of the needle. Bring the needle out at A.

3. Re-insert the needle through the second bar and bring it out at B. Repeat this until the band of straight stitches has been completed. Return to the base of the stitch and repeat the sequence, this time keeping the working thread to the right of the needle.

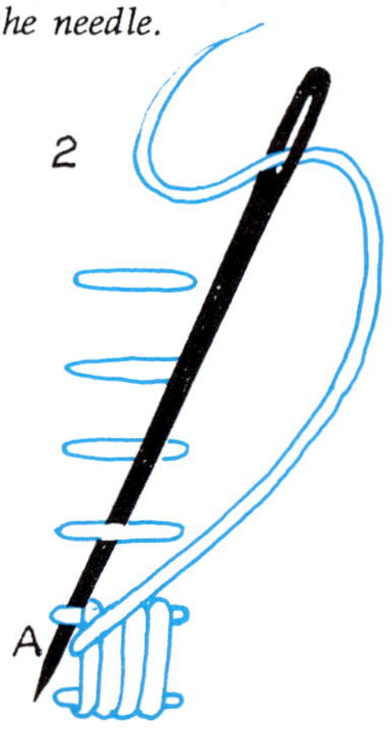

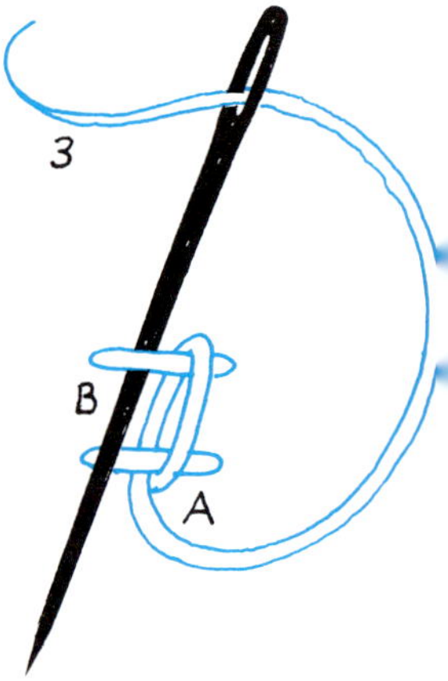

Rose

This is a very pretty stitch which is especially attractive as decoration on children's garments. It is composed of a French knot surrounded by rows of overlapping straight stitches. It is a formal stitch and is thus not particularly suitable for experimentation by altering the scale of the stitches, etc. Rose stitch looks best in a medium-weight thread, especially silks. The central knot could be in a contrasting or toning thread.

1. Work a French knot for the centre of each stitch. Do not pull the threads too tightly.

2. For the straight stitches, bring the needle out at A. Insert it at B and bring out again at C. Continue with this stitch until the knot has been encircled several times. Again, do not pull the stitches too tightly.

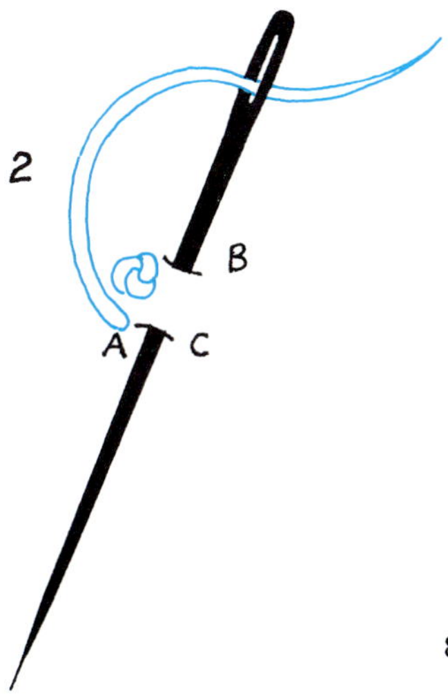

Roumanian

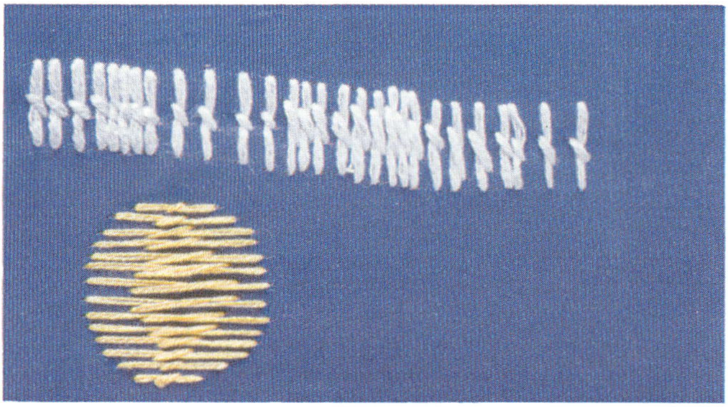

Roumanian stitch can be used both as a border stitch and as a filling stitch for leaves, flowers, etc. It forms a wide solid border if worked traditionally, with the stitches set very close together. They can also be set further apart, although if the stitches are too isolated they look rather strange. Experiment with a variety of threads from fine cotton to thick knitting yarns. The length of the straight stitch can be altered too, setting long stitches beside short stitches.

1. Bring the needle out to the surface at A. Insert it at B and bring out again at C.

2. Re-insert the needle at D and bring out again at E, ready to work the next stitch.

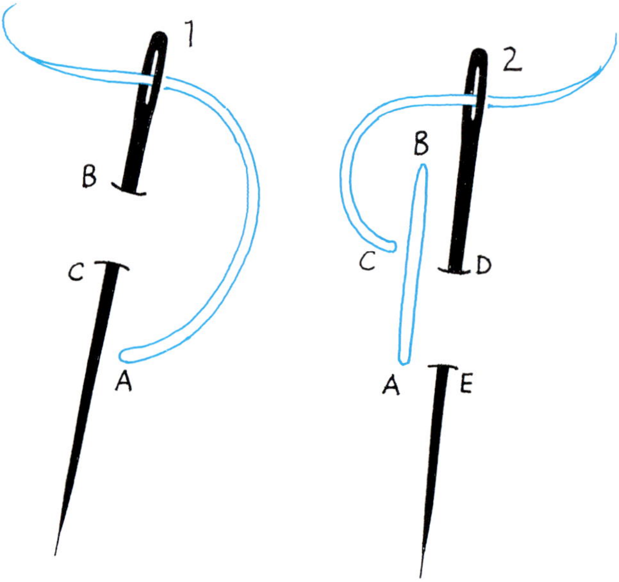

Running

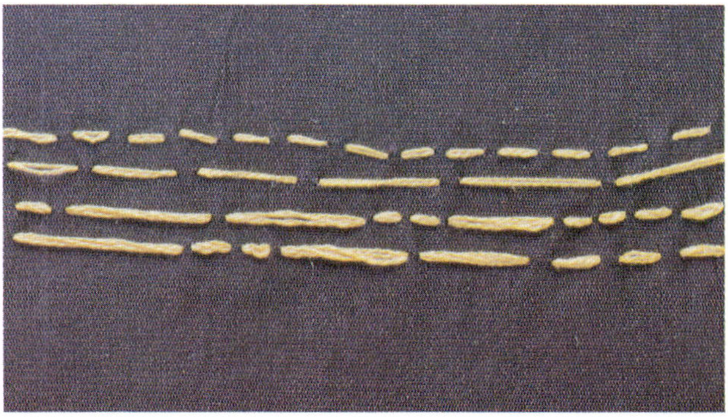

Although a very simple stitch, running stitch is extremely versatile. It is also the main stitch used in quilting. It can be used in all types of embroidery, from traditional work to the wildly experimental. It is useful in landscapes or figurative work, where it can be worked quite freely. It is also useful for building up patterns when worked evenly and regularly. Any type of thread can be used although thicker yarns should be confined to backgrounds with a loose weave. Change the length of the stitch as it is worked, making some stitches very long and others quite short. Vary the length of the spaces between the stitches. Experiment by working rows of running stitch very close together and overlapping some of the rows.

Bring the needle out to the surface at A. Insert it at B and bring out again at C ready to commence the next stitch.

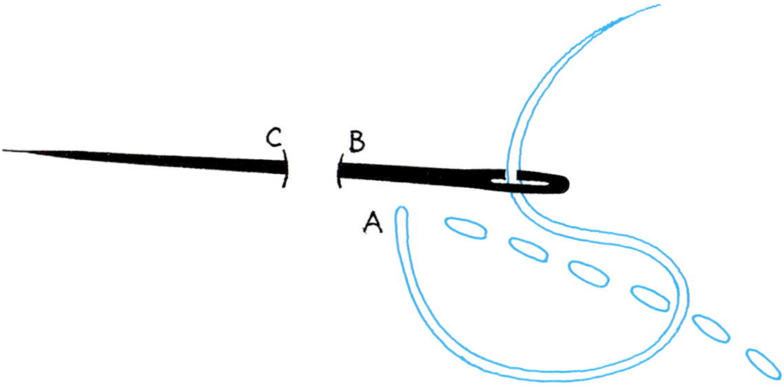

Interlaced Running

Here are just two variations of simple running stitch. Both are useful for patterns or borders. Any weight of smooth threads can be used, from fine machine threads to thick yarns. The interlacing threads can be slightly textured if required. The running stitches are usually set at regular intervals but can be placed close together or further apart to add interest. Use combinations of shiny and matt threads, or contrasting colours.

In both stitches shown here, two parallel rows of running stitches are worked.

1. Without piercing the fabric, and working from left to right, weave the interlacing thread in and out of the stitches as shown in the diagram. A second thread, usually contrasting, is then worked from right to left, filling the spaces (see top line in the photograph).

2. The second stitch is a little more complicated. Without piercing the fabric, and working from left to right, weave the interlacing thread as shown in the diagram (see lower two lines in the photograph).

1

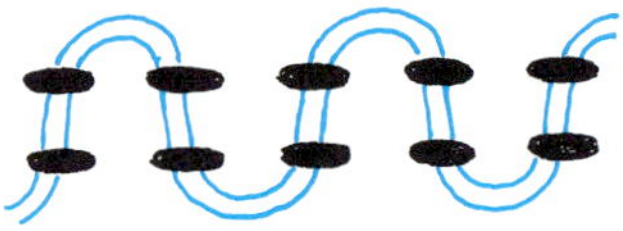

2

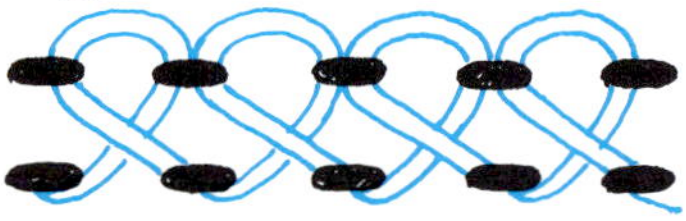

Whipped Running

This variation of simple running stitch, sometimes called cordonnet stitch, forms a more solid line than running stitch, and can be used in all types of embroidery including landscapes and figurative work. Any type of thread can be used, although thicker yarns should be confined to backgrounds with a loose weave. Choose a contrasting or toning thread to whip the running stitch. Vary the length of the stitch as it is worked, making some stitches very long and others quite short, and also vary the length of the space between the stitches.

1. Work a row of running stitches.

2. Thread the needle through the running stitches. The needle should not pierce the fabric. Do not pull the thread too tightly or the stitch will become distorted.

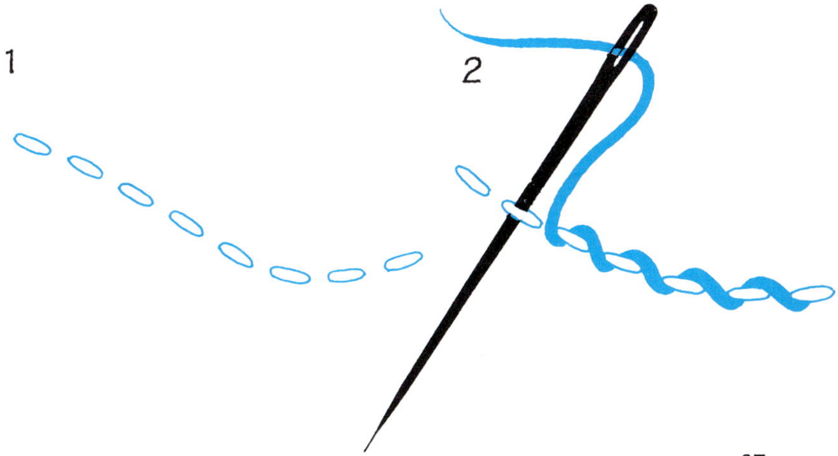

Satin

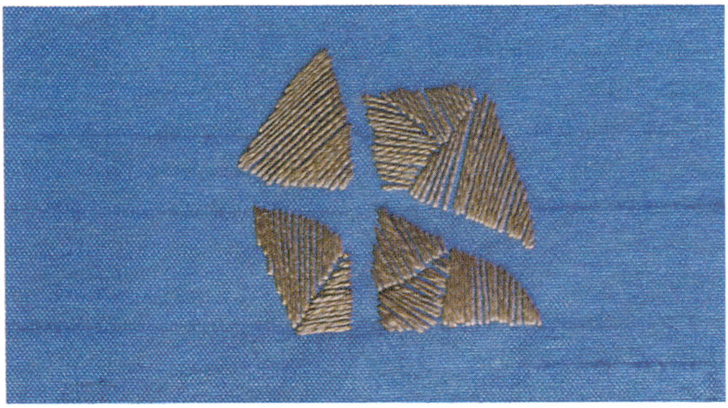

Deceptively simple, practice is needed to achieve a good effect with this stitch. Satin stitch consists of blocks of straight stitches. In adjacent blocks the stitch direction is varied to make the best use of the play of light on the threads. It works particularly well when silk threads are used and especially when one colour is worked throughout. Do not use too long a stitch or the threads will not lie properly and the beauty of the stitch will be lost. If required, the stitch can be worked over card shapes or rows of chain or running stitch to give extra depth to the work.

Bring the needle out to the surface at A and insert at B, which is exactly opposite A. Bring the needle out again at C, very close to A, ready to commence the next stitch.

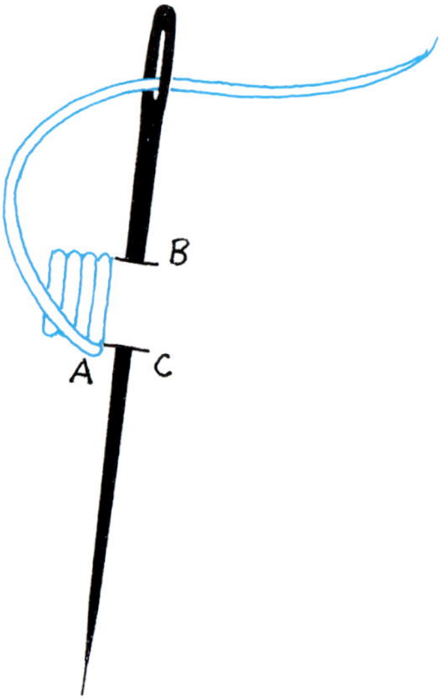

Scroll

Although quite simple, a little practice is needed to work this stitch well. Scroll stitch is best worked in a smooth, medium-weight thread, although finer and heavier threads can be used with good results. Vary the spaces between the stitches, leaving some very wide spaces and then working several stitches close together. Experiment by working rows of scroll stitch very closely together with some of the rows overlapping. Work the stitches of one row in the spaces left by the stitches in the row above. The stitch is worked from left to right.

Bring the needle out to the front of the fabric at A. Insert it at B and bring out again at C, with the working thread looped under the needle as shown in the diagram.

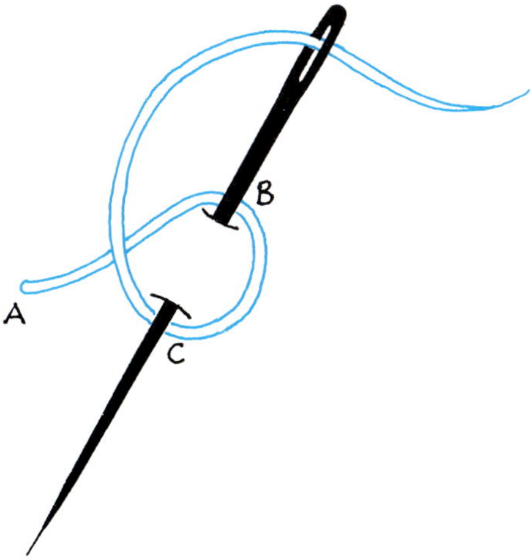

Seeding

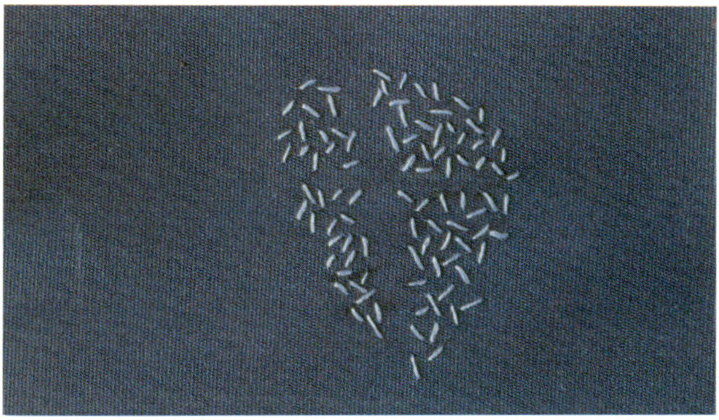

Seeding, a very simple and effective filling stitch, was used in Elizabethan embroidery and is still appropriate in contemporary work. It is often used to give textural interest to an otherwise plain background. Seeding is also useful in voiding, that is, when the main shapes are left unworked and the background is embroidered. It works best in fine or medium-weight threads of all kinds, although thicker yarns can be used where appropriate.

Seeding consists of tiny back stitches worked in all directions. If possible, the stitches should be kept to the same length.

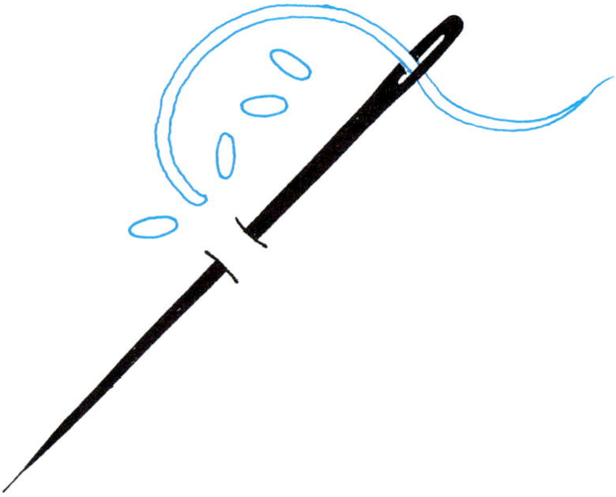

Sheaf Filling

Sheaf stitch is a traditional and attractive stitch consisting of wrapped straight stitches. It is used as a filling stitch and is worked in rows either directly below each other, or in a half drop repeat pattern. It is probably best worked in a medium or fine thread and can be rather overpowering if a thicker thread is used. Sheaf stitch does not lend itself readily to experimentation but interesting effects could be obtained by varying the threads used.

1. *Three straight stitches should first be worked. A tiny space should be left between each stitch.*

2. *Bring the needle out to the front of the fabric at A and wrap the working thread around the stitches as shown, without piercing the fabric. Repeat this last step but this time take the needle through to the back of the fabric, so that each sheaf is wrapped with two horizontal stitches.*

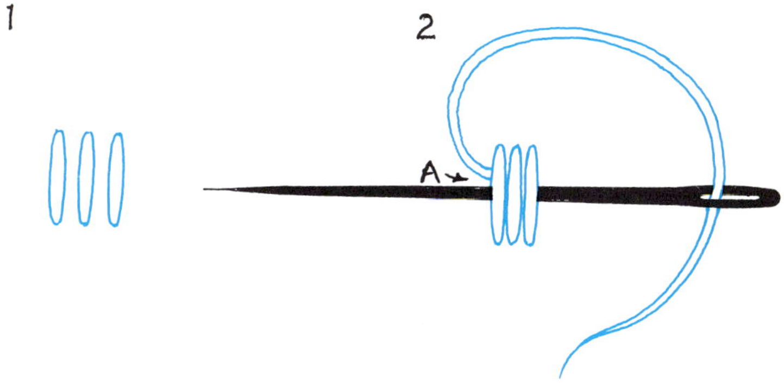

Sorbello

This stitch can be worked either as a line with the stitches set close together, or as a filling stitch, where the stitches will be placed apart and at regular intervals. Smooth medium-weight or thicker threads are best. Finer threads can be used but they make the stitches look very sparse. Twisted cottons or silks work particularly well. Although traditionally worked as a regular repeat pattern or as a linear stitch, sorbello can be massed together to build up textured areas. Use a variety of thicknesses and types of thread.

1. Bring the needle out to the surface at A. Insert at B and bring out again at C.

2. Without piercing the fabric, take the needle under and over the straight stitch. Repeat, with the thread lying under the needle, as shown in the diagram.

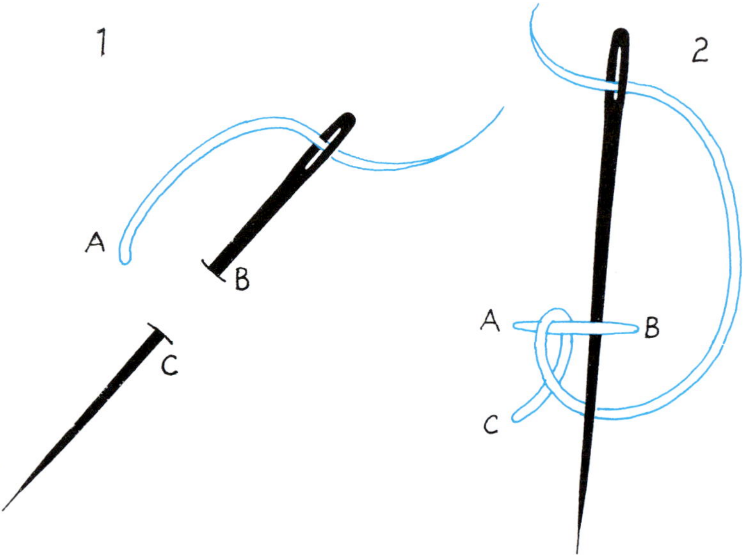

Spider Web

A very raised circular stitch, this is quite simple to work although care is needed to keep the tension even. Spider web is best worked in a smooth, medium-weight thread. Heavier threads can be used, but this will result in a very large stitch. It can work well if a random dyed twisted thread is used. The stitch does not lend itself readily to experimentation but interesting effects can be achieved by varying the colours and types of threads used.

Before working the stitch, it is a good idea to mark the outline of a circle on the fabric.

1. *Work a foundation of four straight stitches, as diameters of a circle.*

2. *Bring the needle out at the centre of the circle. Without piercing the fabric, take the needle back over and under one spoke of the wheel and then forward under the next spoke, as shown in the diagram. This stitch is repeated until the spokes have all been covered.*

1

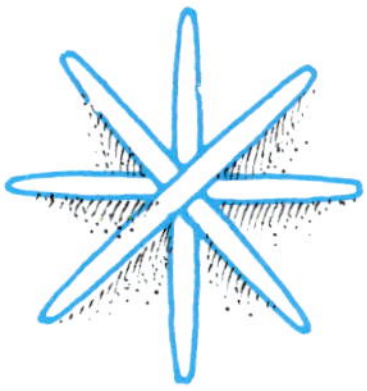

2

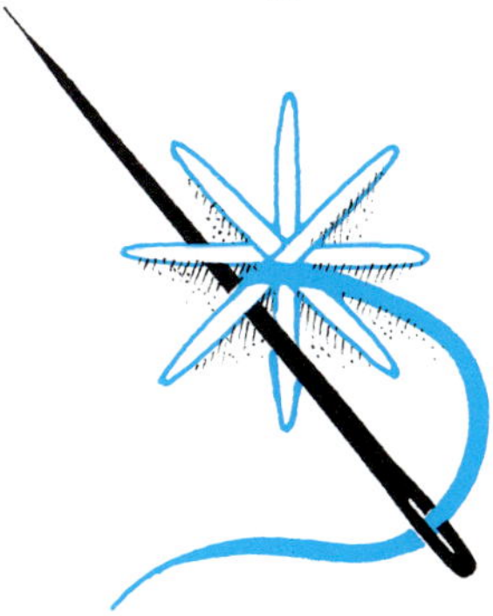

Split

This is not a difficult stitch to work, although care should be taken over the choice of thread used. Split stitch was very popular in medieval embroideries (for example, the Opus Anglicanum) where it was used to work faces, often in spiralling pattern. It is not much used in modern embroidery, although it is still useful when a fine, curved line is required. Fine and medium-weight soft threads are most suitable (tightly twisted threads will be very difficult to work effectively).

Bring the needle out to the surface at A and insert it at B. Bring the needle out again at C and insert the point through the working thread. Pull the needle carefully through the thread taking care that the thread is not damaged.

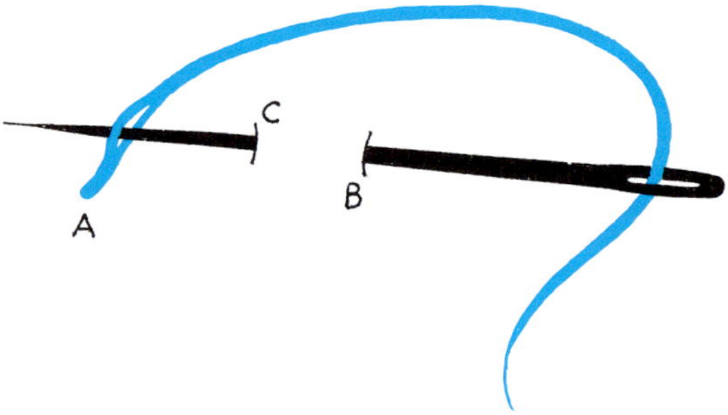

Star Filling

A powdered filling stitch, which is effective and very simple to work, each stitch consisting of a series of cross stitches worked on top of each other. Star filling stitch is most often used as an overall background pattern, with the stitches placed at regular intervals. However, it is also interesting if stitched unevenly, perhaps with stitches placed very close together or encroaching on each other, and of varying sizes, to build up patterns. Any type of thread may be used, and parts of each stitch could be worked in different threads if desired.

1. *Start with an upright cross.*
2. *For the next stage, work a diagonal cross over the upright cross.*
3. *Finally, work a small cross stitch on top.*

Stem

Very similar to outline stitch, stem stitch is simple to work and produces a fine line, often used in floral embroideries to work foliage. Any type of thread may be used, from fine sewing cottons and crewel wools to thick knitting yarns. Experiment with a variety of threads ranging from shiny to matt. Vary the length of each stitch, making some stitches very short and others very long. Work lines of stitches so that they encroach on and cross over each other.

The method of working is the same as for outline stitch, except that the working thread is always kept to the right of the needle. It is usually worked upwards.

Bring the needle out through the fabric at A. Insert it at B and bring out again at C ready to commence the next stitch.

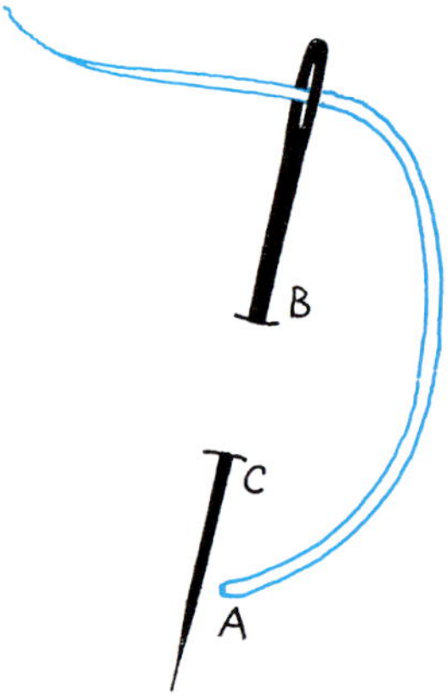

Raised Stem Band

This forms a solid raised border that is quite simple to work. Firm, medium-weight threads are best but thicker yarns could be used. Traditionally, the foundation threads are completely covered by the stem stitches, but it is possible to space the rows of stem stitches so that the core threads are seen, if desired. Contrasting or toning threads can equally well be used, and shiny and matt threads of the same colour also look good. Vary the space between the horizontal stitches, placing some of the stitches very close together and others well apart. Work the stem stitches in different threads.

1. A row of long straight stitches is first laid down. These stitches must be packed close together.

2. Next, a row of equally spaced horizontal stitches is worked over the core threads.

3. Rows of stem stitches are then worked over this foundation. The needle does not pierce the fabric at this stage but is inserted into each horizontal stitch in turn (see stem stitch for working instructions).

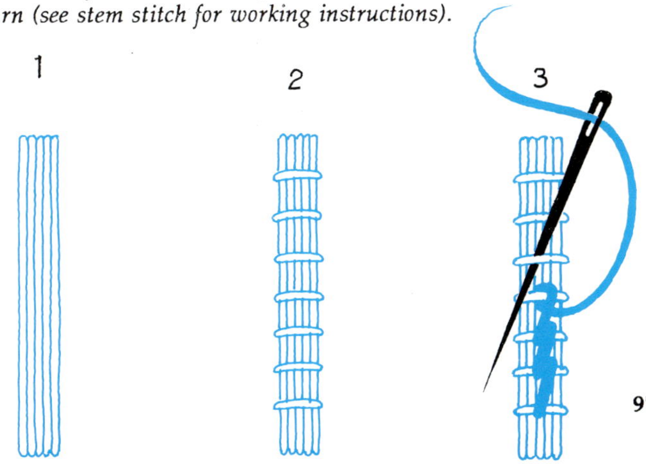

Whipped Stem

This is a variation of stem stitch, producing a much bolder line of stitchery. Any type of thread may be used, from fine sewing cottons and crewel wools to thick yarns. Experiment with a variety of threads, shiny and matt, and use a different thread for each part of the stitch. As with stem stitch, vary the length of each stitch, making some very short and others very long, and work lines of stitches so that they encroach on each other. The finished effect will be much more textured than when using simple stem stitch.

1. *Work a row of stem stitch.*

2. *Take another thread under and over each stitch as shown in the diagram. The needle should not pierce the fabric.*

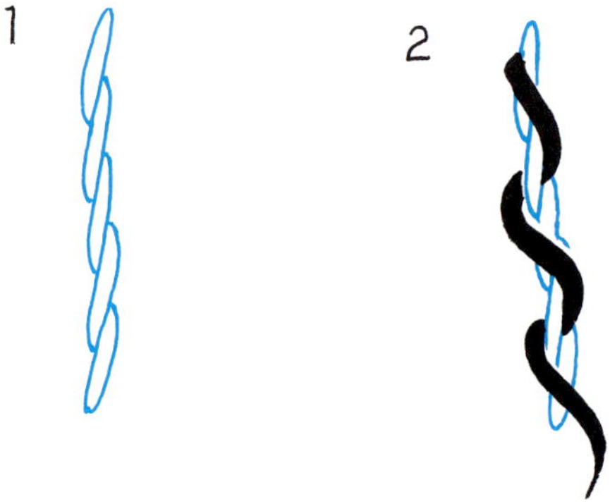

Straight

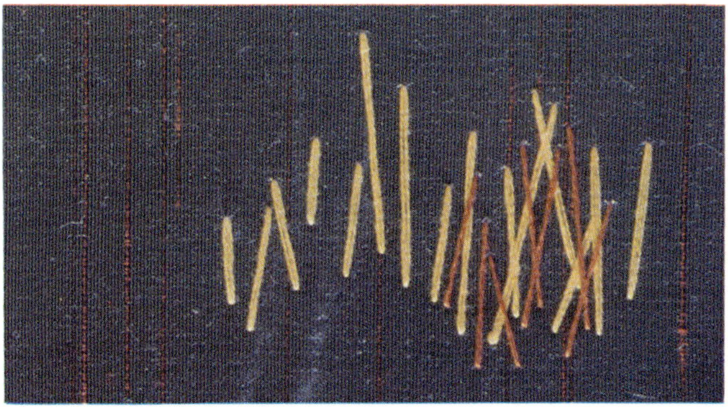

As its name implies, straight stitch is the simplest yet one of the most versatile of stitches. It is often used in contemporary embroidery because it can be worked very freely. Any type of thread may be used, from very fine sewing cottons and metallic threads to thick knitting yarns or torn or cut strips of fabric. The stitch may be worked in any length, but beware of using too long a stitch if working embroidery that is to be used (cushions, etc.) as the thread may catch and break. Build up very textured areas by working the stitches on top of each other in a wide variety of threads, varying the colours and textures.

Bring the needle out to the surface at A. Insert at B and bring out again at C ready to commence the next stitch.

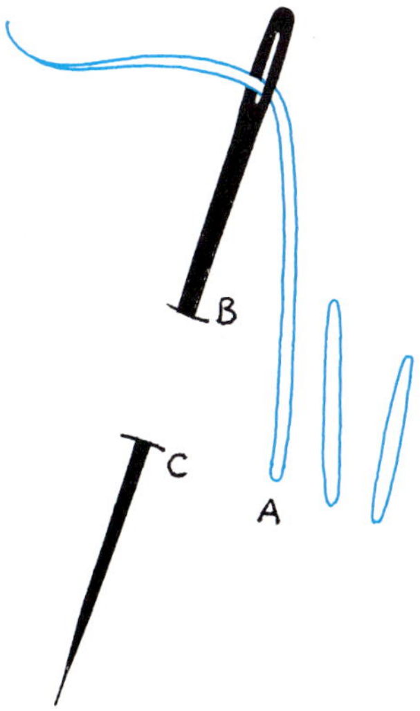

Tete-de-Boeuf

Tete-de-boeuf stitch is a pretty filling stitch which can be used successfully on children's clothes. It is usually worked as an overall background pattern with the stitches set in rows in a half drop repeat pattern. It is best suited to this somewhat formal pattern and some of its charm may be lost if used too experimentally. It is, however, a very attractive stitch and should not be overlooked, as it it useful for working formal patterns and some floral embroideries. A fine or medium-weight thread is best to use.

1. *The first part of the stitch is a detached chain stitch.*
2. *Work two small, straight diagonal stitches as shown in the diagram.*

LEFT ***Tulips in the park*** *worked by Vicky Lugg, a small panel worked entirely by hand. The sky and the flowers are all in straight stitches using a variety of threads. The trees are worked in French knots and seeding stitch. Embroidered area: 2 x 6.5 inches (5 x 16 cm).*

Thorn

Thorn stitch is a simple and versatile stitch, although care is needed to maintain the correct tension. It is a type of couching in which the couched thread is stitched down by the working thread and a 'thorn-like' stitch produced. Any type of thread may be used, from fine sewing cottons and crewel wools to thick knitting yarns, although care is needed when using very thick threads. Vary the position of the crossed stitches, working some very close together and others much further apart. Work lines of stitches on top of each other at varying angles to build up a rich textured surface.

The first part of the stitch consists of a long, straight stitch and care should be taken to ensure that the thread lies flat on the surface.

1. Bring the needle out to the surface at A. Insert it at B and bring out again at C.

2. Re-insert the needle at D, and bring out again at E.

3. Insert the needle again at F and bring out again at G ready to commence the next stitch.

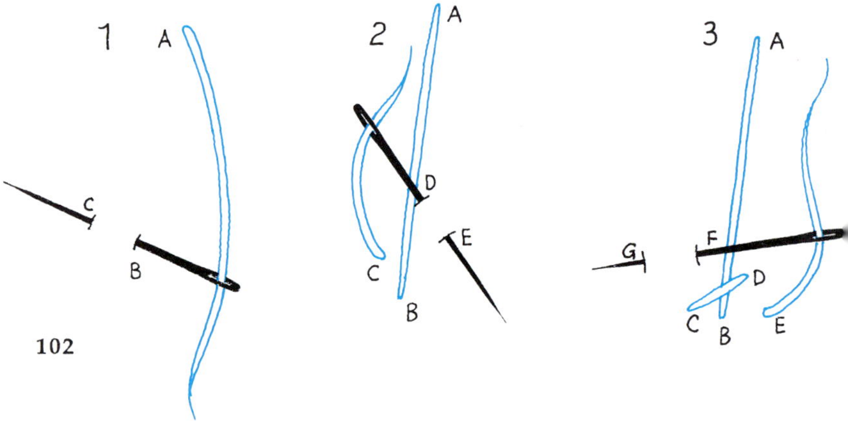

Trailing

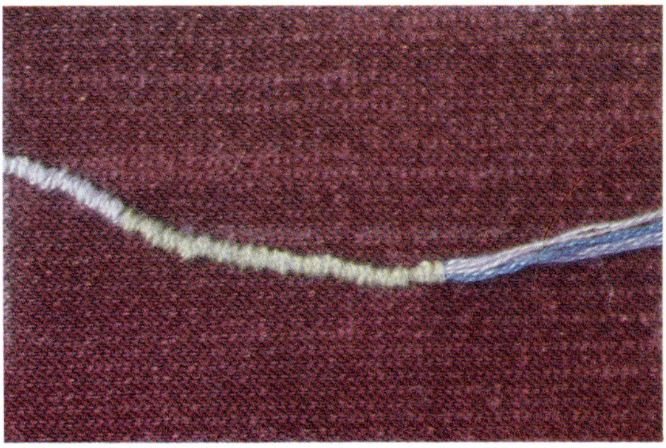

This stitch is often known as satin couching stitch. It is very effective although not a particularly easy stitch to work.

A bundle of threads is laid down on the surface of the fabric and covered in small satin stitches. This produces a ridged outline stitch similar to overcasting but much more raised in texture. The core threads are usually completely covered in stitchery but areas could be left uncovered if desired, and a variety of smooth threads could be used in different colours, or even metallic threads. The ends of the core threads could be snipped and left like tassels on the fabric surface when the stitch is complete. A fairly fine, smooth thread should be used for the couching thread, but the core threads could be of any smooth thread, and the thicker the bundle the more raised the finished stitch will be.

The stitch is usually worked from left to right. Lay the core threads on the surface of the fabric, securing them firmly at the left hand edge of the work. Bring the needle out through the fabric at A. Insert it at B and bring out again at C ready to commence the next stitch.

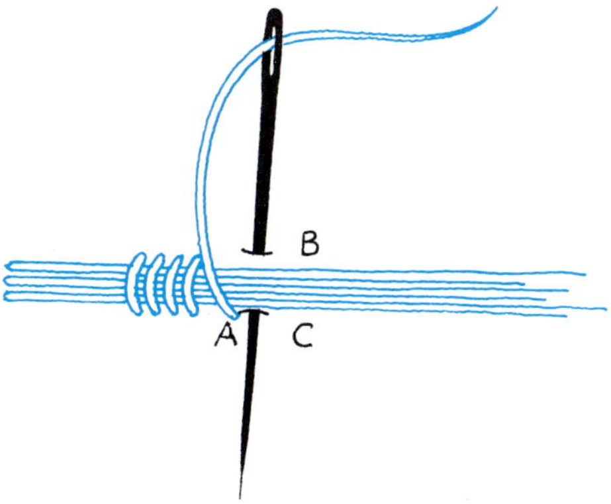

Van Dyke

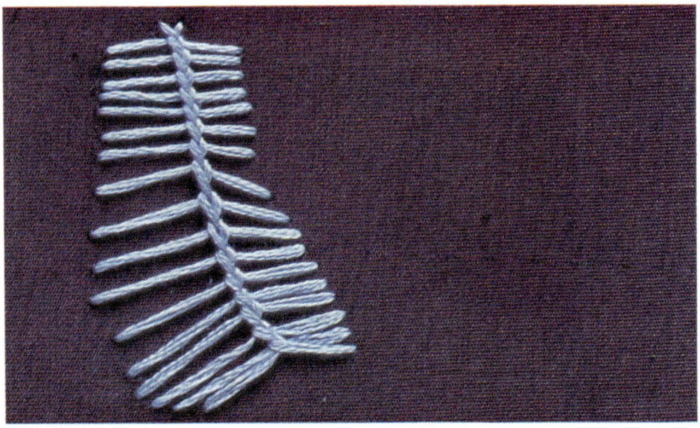

This forms an effective raised border stitch. It is best worked in a smooth medium-weight thread, although finer or thicker threads could be used and more surface interest obtained by contrasting matt and shiny threads. It forms a thick, plaited band which can be used when building geometric patterns. Experiment with the stitches, working some close together and others further apart, which will result in the line becoming curved and more interesting in texture. The stitch is usually worked from top to bottom.

1. *Bring the needle out at A. Insert it at B and bring out again at C.*

2. *Re-insert the needle at D and bring out again at E ready to commence the next stitch. Note: This instruction is for the first stitch only.*

3. *For the next and every subsequent stitch, the needle should pass through the crossed threads (at CB on the diagram) without piercing the fabric. (In this stitch the needle will enter the fabric again at F, forming a new cross below CB).*

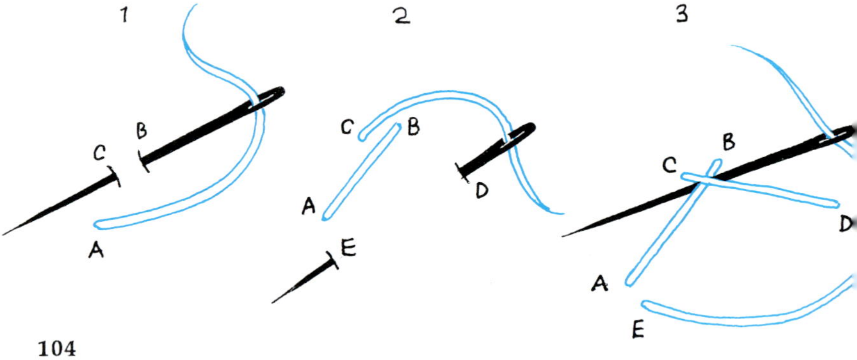

Cowes Week A small panel worked entirely in straight stitch. The silk background fabric has been spattered with blue fabric paint. The sea is worked in silk threads and the sails of the yachts in triangles of straight stitches. Embroidered area: 4.5 x 6.5 inches (11.5 x 16.5 cm).

Wave

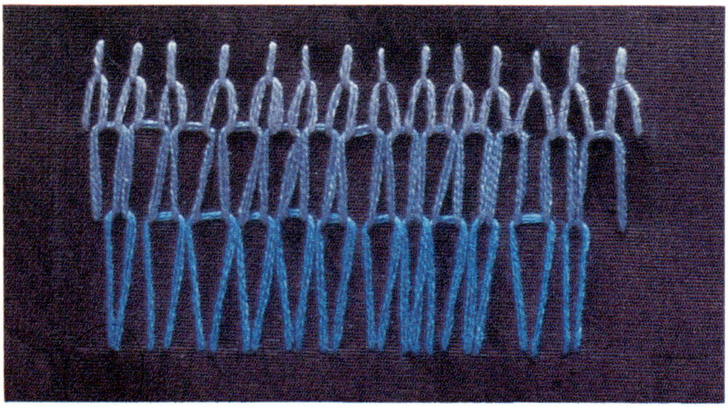

As it can be worked quite quickly, this is a useful stitch for covering background areas. Any smooth medium-weight thread can be used although thicker or finer threads can all be used with good effect. Silk threads work particularly well. It is possible to build up shaded areas by using a toning range of colours. Experiment with the spacing of the stitches: if they are worked close together a finely patterned area will emerge; if the rows are spaced further apart the stitch will be more open and lacy in appearance.

1. *Work a row of small vertical straight stitches, evenly spaced apart.*
2. *For the next row, bring the needle out to the surface at A. Pass the needle through two of the stitches in the first row without piercing the fabric.*
3. *Re-insert the needle through the fabric at B and bring out again at C ready to commence the next stitch. In subsequent rows the needle will be taken through two stitches of the row above.*

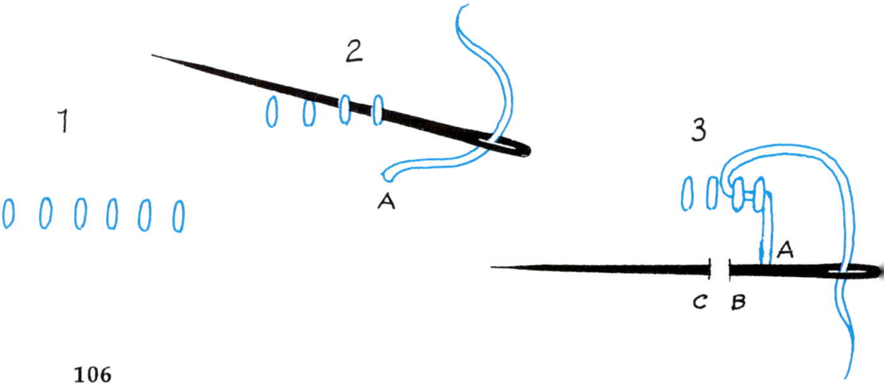

Wheat Ear

This is a very simple stitch, effective as a border or all-over texture, useful when working landscapes or floral embroideries. Any type of thread may be used, from very fine sewing cottons and metallic threads to thick knitting yarns, although the stitch lends itself well to finer threads. A variety of textures can be obtained by working lines of stitches on top of each other in a wide variety of threads, varying the colours and textures. Although it looks complicated it is, in fact, very easy to work. The stitch is usually worked from top to bottom.

1. *Bring the needle out through to the surface at A, insert it at B and bring out again at C.*
2. *Re-insert the needle at A and bring out again at D.*
3. *Take the needle through the two stitches at A, without piercing the fabric, and re-insert at D, forming a loop.*

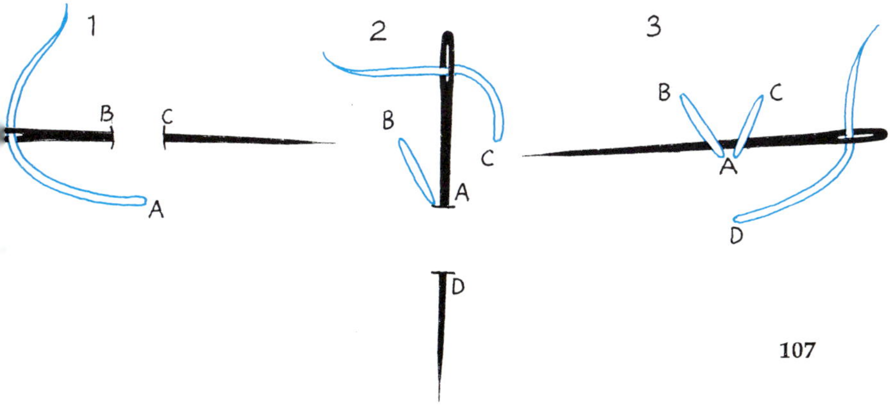

Detached Wheat Ear

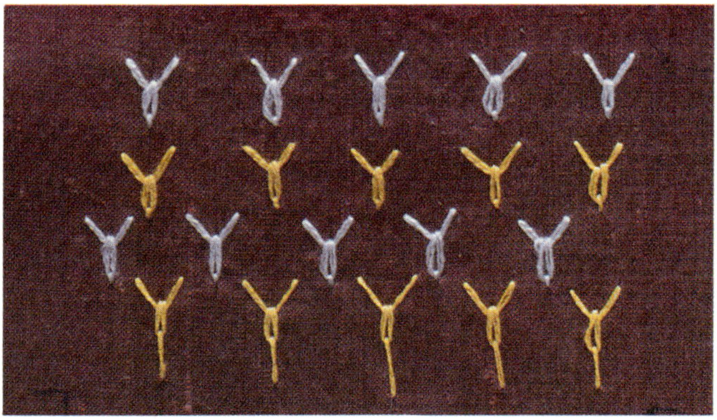

This is a charming isolated stitch, commonly used as an all-over pattern. It is in fact a combination of arrowhead stitch and detached chain stitch, and is much easier to work than it looks. It can be worked in any thread from fine cotton to thick yarns, although it is probably more successful in a fine or medium-weight thread. The spaces between the stitches could be varied, some stitches worked close together and some far apart to give more interest. This stitch lends itself well to the interpretation of gardens and flowers as, when worked in fine threads, it looks very like a flower or seed head.

1. *Bring the needle out through the fabric at A. Insert the needle at B and bring out again at C.*
2. *Insert the needle again at B to form a V shape, and bring out again at D, immediately above B.*
3. *Re-insert the needle at D and bring out at E with the working thread lying under the needle.*
4. *Insert the needle into the fabric at E and bring out again at F, ready to work the next stitch.*

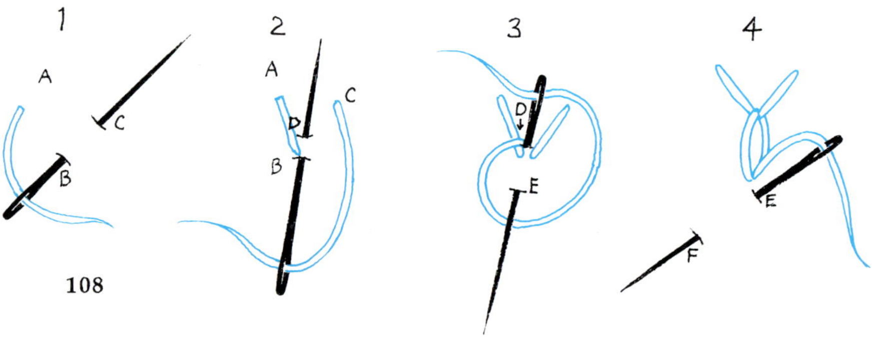

Zig Zag

Zig zag stitch is a simple geometric stitch which forms an effective border. Any smooth thread can be used, although care should be taken if thicker yarns are used so that the effect is not overwhelming. It looks particularly good in twisted silks or cottons. To add more surface interest, the cross stitches can be varied in width; some very narrow and others quite wide. It is very effective when building up patterns or rich borders, and works well in metallic threads on a dark fabric.

The stitch is worked in two stages.

1. Working from right to left, bring the needle out through the fabric at A. Insert it at B and bring out again at A.

2. Insert at C and bring out again at D. Repeat this until the line of stitching has been worked. To complete the cross stitches, this time working from left to right, bring the needle out at D, insert it at B and bring out again at A.

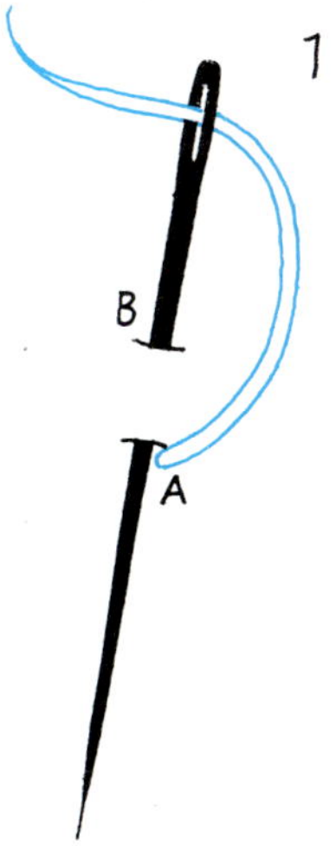

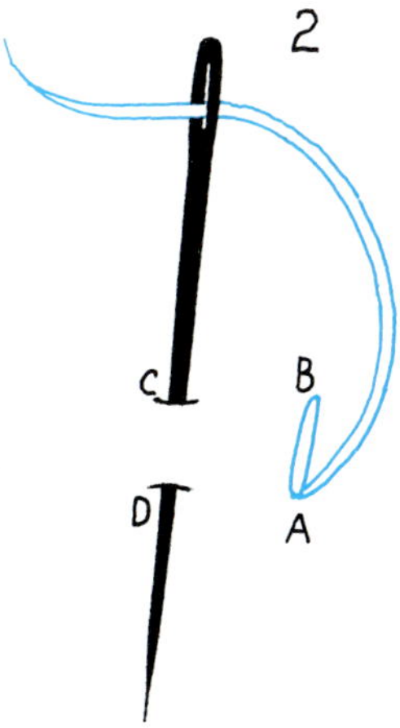

List of stitches by type

Alphabetical list of stitches

Bibliography

Beaney, Jan *The Art of the Needle*, London 1988
Best, Muriel *The Needlework School*, Bromley 1984
Bullen, Jenny *Starting Embroidery*, London 1989
Butler, Anne *The Batsford Encyclopaedia of Embroidery Stitches*, London 1979
Campbell-Harding, Valerie and Pam Watts *Machine Embroidery: Stitch Techniques*, London 1989
Embroiderers Guild, *Embroidery* Magazine, published quarterly
Thomas, Mary *Dictionary of Embroidery Stitches*, London 1936, 1986

Suppliers

Madeira manufacture a most extensive and comprehensive range of high quality hand and machine embroidery threads for handicraft use, including 4 strand pure silk, 6 strand cotton floss, mercerised and fast-dyed 100% cotton, viscose rayon and 100% polyester threads in a range of different counts. Madeira also produce many different metallic threads, including those for cord embroidery and knitting, and are constantly expanding their range.

However, as is suggested in this book, there is no limit to the range of threads, knitting wools, strips of fabric etc., which can be used in surface embroidery. Many of these products are available in your local craft, specialist thread, wool and fabric shops.

Suppliers of Madeira Threads

UNITED KINGDOM

A full list of suppliers in the United Kingdom and other English-speaking countries is available on request from Madeira Threads (UK) Ltd, Thirsk Industrial Park, York Road, Thirsk, North Yorkshire YO7 3BX.

EUROPE

Madeira Garne
U. & M. Schmidt & Co. GmbH
Hans Buntestr 8
D-7800 FREIBURG
WEST GERMANY

AUSTRALIA

Penguin Threads Pty Ltd
25-27 Izett Street
PRAHAN 3181
Victoria

USA

Madeira USA Ltd
30 Bayside Court
LACONIA
New Hampshire 03246

Madeira USA Ltd (West Coast)
2727 N. Grove Industrial Drive
FRESNO
California 93727